Designing MIT:
Bosworth's New Tech

Designing MIT

Bosworth's New Tech

Mark Jarzombek

NORTHEASTERN UNIVERSITY PRESS

Northeastern University Press

Library of Congress Cataloging-in-Publication Data
Jarzombek, Mark.
  Designing MIT : Bosworth's New Tech / Mark Jarzombek.
     p. cm.
  Includes bibliographical references and index.
  ISBN 1-55553-619-0 (cloth : alk. paper)
1. Massachusetts Institute of Technology—Buildings—Design and construction. 2. Bosworth, Welles, 1869–1966. I. Title.
T171.M475 2004
727'.3'097444—dc22   2004009736

Designed by Janis Owens, Books By Design, Inc.

Composed in Minion by Books By Design, Inc., in Cambridge, Massachusetts.

Printed and bound by Friesens, Altona, Manitoba, Canada. The paper is Jenson Satin, an acid-free sheet.

MANUFACTURED IN CANADA
09   08   07   06   05   04   5   4   3   2   1

Contents

Preface

On June 13, 1916, Boston witnessed a spectacular public event unlike anything ever staged in the city: an outdoor, evening performance in MIT's new Grand Court celebrating the opening of the New Tech. On that evening, Virginia Tanner and her troupe, accompanied by dozens of actors, a chorus of 500 singers, and an orchestra of 100 musicians, performed "The Masque of Power." The performance was attended by such dignitaries as Alexander Graham Bell, Orville Wright, Henry Cabot Lodge, and Franklin Delano Roosevelt. Today, almost 100 years later, the MIT building stands largely unchanged, testifying to the energy and farsighted planning of a number of men, many of them MIT graduates, who rose to the occasion and took up the challenges of the new age.

Although several books on the history of the MIT campus have been published, there is little information available about the design of the main MIT academic building, which along with the Walker Memorial, the President's House, and the dormitory known as Senior House, was part of the initial building campaign. Consequently, when I researched the MIT archives, I hoped at best to find perhaps a few letters and some construction drawings. Instead I was surprised to discover quite a dramatic story as MIT, originally founded in 1861, had to rethink its institutional identity when it decided to move away from its cramped quarters in the Back Bay. The documents I found detailed the struggle to find a suitable architectural expression for one of the preeminent institutions of the United States. The process was shepherded to a successful completion to no small degree because of the leadership of MIT's young and energetic president, Richard Maclaurin. In the series of architectural projects that were forwarded and the various architects that were consulted we can now follow, step by step, the various phases of the process. Unlike other institutions making commissions of this scale at that time, MIT went through several architects before deciding on William Welles Bosworth. There were, among an assortment of unsigned proposals, designs by Stephen Child, a student of Frederick Law Olmsted; Désiré Despradelle, a Frenchman trained at the École des Beaux-Arts; John R. Freeman, an MIT-trained civil engineer; and finally, Bosworth, who came with high recommendations from John D. Rockefeller Jr. and Theodore Newton Vail, the president of AT&T. The irony is that none of these architects had any particular expertise in campus design, and it was perhaps on account of this that the New Tech, as it was called, came to be so uniquely—and so successfully—tailored to the needs and ambitions of MIT.

The period from the 1890s to World War I was an astonishing time in American architecture, with campus design, after skyscrapers, the preeminent area of innovation. The campuses of Princeton, West Point, Stanford, and the University of Washington, among others, are still today testaments to the creativity and vision of that era. MIT, however, differed in many respects and struck its own path. Unlike these other institutions of learning, it was not only resolutely urban, but also an important element in Boston's emerging neoclassical silhouette. Furthermore, under the gentle prodding of its architect, the MIT building came to reflect an amazingly successful and unique synthesis of motifs. Its Ionic exterior harkened to the ideals of Greek civilization; its dome, based on the Pantheon in Rome, was a symbol of the unity of knowledge; its overall organization reflected the Beaux-Arts traditions of Bosworth's training; and its plan was modeled on the leading German academic buildings of the time. Finally, the concrete construction technique that was used anticipated by a number of years the age of modern architecture. The MIT building is thus without equal in the American architectural context. It has become an icon in its own right and, above all, at a time when the river's edge in Boston, as elsewhere in the United States, was seen as little more than a place to locate highways, it was the only building in Boston that could rightly claim to be a part of the Charles River landscape.

This book is not the history of MIT proper or of the post-Bosworthian campus. For that I ask readers to consult the bibliography for titles of works that deal with those subjects. I also recommend Henry Greenleaf Pearson's *Richard Cockburn Maclaurin, President of the Massachusetts Institute of Technology, 1909–1920,* Samuel Cate Prescott's *When M.I.T. Was "Boston Tech," 1861–1916,* and Francis E. Wylie's *MIT in Perspective, a Pictorial History of the Massachusetts Institute of Technology.*

There are many people I would like to thank for their help with this book. My deepest gratitude to Charles M. Vest, president of MIT, for his encouragement. I thank William Mitchell, dean of MIT's School of Architecture and Planning; Terry Knight, acting dean of the School of Architecture and Planning; and Stanford Anderson, head of the Department of Architecture of MIT. I am especially grateful for their unwavering belief in the timeliness of this book. Among the numerous librarians and archivists who generously donated their time and helped me with various aspects of my research, my thanks to Mary Eleanor Murphy, MIT Archives; Gary A. Van Zante and Jenny

O'Neill, curators at the MIT Museum; Pat Watson of the New Britain Public Library; Donzella Maupin of the Hampton University Archives; Robert Roache of the Shepley Bulfinch Archives; Marjorie Strong of the Vermont Historical Society; Kimberly Alexander of the Peabody and Essex Museum; Michael Dosch, Frederick Law Olmsted Archives; Sheldon Hochheiser, Corporate Historian at AT&T; Abigail Martin, Joint Free Public Library of Morristown and Morris Township; and Eunice Haugen, the Minnesota Museum of American Art. My gratitude also goes to MIT student Ken Giesekie, who helped with the scanning of the images.

I thank in particular Gail Fenske, Elizabeth Grossman, and Richard Chafee, from whom I received warm support and experienced advice. I would also like to thank Douglass Shand-Tucci for so generously sharing with me his extensive knowledge of the history of Boston architecture.

Designing MIT:
Bosworth's New Tech

part one

From the Rogers Building to the New Tech

The Changing Identity of MIT: Why the Move?

When the Massachusetts Institute of Technology received its charter in 1861, the streets of Boston's Back Bay were still in the process of being laid out along the once swampy shore of the Charles River. On the vast flat tract of land there soon would arise an urban landscape of elegant boulevards and uniform row houses. To maximize this unique opportunity and to contribute to a vibrant cultural community, the city earmarked several of the new lots for churches, museums, and other public buildings, with the first such lot—an entire city block between Boylston and Newbury streets—given over to the Natural History Society and the newly founded MIT.[1] The creation of the Institute and the allocation of such a prestigious site were major victories for MIT's founder, William Barton Rogers (1804–1882), who had worked tirelessly for more than a decade to convince the state legislature to issue a grant for a scientific and technical institution for Boston. Rogers hoped that MIT would get two buildings, one dedicated to the Institute proper and another to serve as a teaching museum where the latest advancements in technology and industrial design would be displayed.

The project was entrusted to the French-trained Bostonian architect William G. Preston, who placed the more conservative of the institutions, the Natural History Society building, on the narrow side of the lot, and MIT in the middle facing Boylston Street [1].[2] The buildings were envisioned as an interconnected ensemble set back from the sidewalk, this being the first and quite possibly the last time that an entire Boston city block was conceived as a unity. The work on the Natural History Society building proceeded quickly, and the building was finished in 1862. The MIT building, later to be named the Rogers Building, opened its doors in 1865, construction having been slowed because of the Civil War.[3] Funding for the MIT teaching museum, however, never materialized, and the site was temporarily left empty. Although Rogers's ambition of an entire city block dedicated to science and the advancement of knowledge faltered, the idea of a museum dedicated to design did not die. In 1871 construction began on the Museum of Fine Arts one block away on Huntington Avenue. (It was eventually torn down to make way for the Copley Hotel.)

The Rogers Building was a five-story-high rectangular structure sporting a grand tetra-style Corinthian portico at the top of a broad flight of steps. Its

1

1 Plan for the MIT Museum: at top, the MIT buildings and the building for the Natural History Society; at bottom, elevation of connecting passageway, William G. Preston, ca. 1861.

design impetus harkened back to the Duke of Wellington's fashionable Apsley House in London, which had been remodeled with such a portico in 1828 by the architect Benjamin Dean Wyatt [2, 3, 4].[4] At the time, the Apsley House was most certainly a suitable prototype, expressing self-confident mastery and the gentlemanly pursuit of excellence. But the sciences were in the process of change, and the atmosphere evoked by the Rogers Building soon became obsolete. By the 1880s, technologies were developing at a rapid pace, professional societies were springing up, and industrialization was expanding. MIT suddenly and fortuitously found itself at the very hub of these events. New faculty members were added and new courses created: the School of Mechanical Arts was established in 1876, and in the same year, the Women's Chemistry Laboratory.[5] The Department of Electrical Engineering was created in 1882, the Department of Chemical Engineering in 1888, and in the 1890s, the Department of Sanitary Engineering was established. The Department of Mining Engineering became

2

FAÇADE.

autonomous and was separated from Geology. A Department of Naval Architecture was founded in 1901. Graduate programs in the various sciences also came into existence. All in all, by the late 1890s, the original cast of 10 faculty and 70 students had ballooned into 150 faculty and 1,300 students.

Already MIT's first expansion, the "Annex," a one-story structure on the vacant lot next to the Rogers Building, was built according to all the rules of advanced laboratory design [5]. Though a seemingly humble one-story building, it was modeled on a Russian factory that had been exhibited at the 1876 Centennial Exposition at Philadelphia and that had been deemed suitable to MIT's needs by a special delegation to the Exposition headed by MIT's president, John D. Runkle.[6] But the Annex was no sooner finished than it was overwhelmed by demand for yet more space, and so in 1886 it was torn down and replaced by the five-story Walker Memorial building that housed the chemistry and physics laboratories [6].[7] Named after MIT's second president, Francis Amasa Walker, it was designed by the German-born Carl Fehmer (1838–1916).[8] The Walker was a full-fledged laboratory building with state-of-the-art ventilation chimneys running up along the façade. The building was, however, not

2 Preliminary drawing of the front elevation of the MIT building, William G. Preston, ca. 1861.

3

4

3 The Rogers Building and, in the foreground, the Natural History Society shortly after construction, ca. 1866.
4 Engraving of the Apsley House, Robert Adam, 1771–1778; façade, Benjamin Dean Wyatt, 1828.

5

6

without its architectural merit, except that its fireproof brick-clad surfaces, numerous windows, and the arcade-motif at the street level, not untypical for warehouse and mercantile buildings in that era, would have been more suited to a factory district than to a site that was the visual end-piece of the Huntington Avenue intersection with Boylston. Given that Fehmer had designed the fashionable Boston residence of Massachusetts governor Oliver Ames, which still exists and is located at the corner of Massachusetts and Commonwealth avenues, the choice of this style, even for such a prominent urban space, was clearly MIT's and a testament to its desire to promote the ideals of scientific professionalism.

The unrelenting demand for ever more space necessitated the construction in 1889 of the imposing six-story Engineering Building "A" on Trinity Place, three blocks from the Rogers, and, attached to it in 1892, Engineering Building "B," also called the Henry L. Pierce Building [7]. Although the buildings are spectacular examples of advanced industrial architecture, no record as to their designer has survived. In the following year, the Institute built Engineering Building "C," which formed a long, L-shaped complex, and finally, a small gymnasium was erected on Exeter Street, some two blocks beyond Trinity Square. The Mechanical Laboratories were eventually relocated to Garrison Street. As a result of this hectic expansion, MIT buildings were spread out over numerous city blocks. For students and faculty, the dispersal of the various faculties was time-consuming and inconvenient [8]. As William Welles Bosworth, the future architect of the new campus and at that time a student at MIT, recalled, "Just going from the old Walker building to the old main building for different classes, without an overcoat, in winter, was cruel."[9]

The absence of dormitories contributed to this sense of diffusion. Students lived in their own apartments or with relatives. If wealthier, they joined social or dining clubs, an arrangement adopted from the German university system.[10] MIT did its best to create a student union, but at first could do no better than to set up a lunchroom in the basement of the Rogers Building. Eventually some rooms in the Mechanical Laboratory building on Garrison Street were renovated for student use. In 1908, there was a glimmer of hope that Copley Hall, then called Grundmann Studios, could be transformed into a Union [9]. Located on Clarendon Street and next to Engineering "A," it was owned by MIT but had been rented out to the Copley Society for artist studios and exhibition spaces.[11] Rather than evict the community of artists, MIT decided to build a new Student Union between the Pierce Building and Engineering "C." Again, the concept was inadequate and fell short of the need.

5 Photograph of "The Annex," ca. 1876.
6 View east along Huntington Avenue with MIT's Walker and Rogers buildings, and the Natural History Society, ca. 1890.

7

7 Engineering Buildings "A"
and "B," looking south along
Trinity Place, ca. 1892.

8

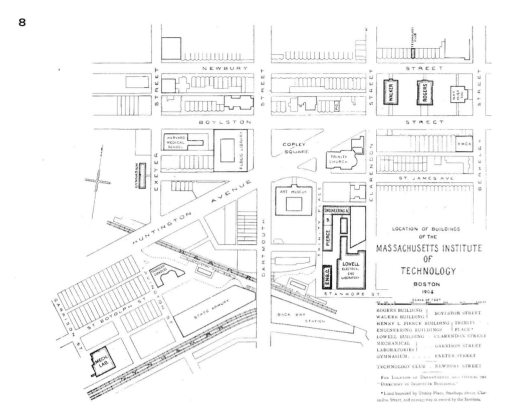

9

8 Site plan showing locations of MIT buildings in Boston, 1904.
9 Photograph of the Grundmann Studio building, looking south along Clarendon Street, ca. 1908.

10

10 View north along Trinity Place with Engineering Building "C" in the foreground and the Student Union and Engineering Building "B" in the background, ca. 1910.

Although elegantly outfitted, it was only two stories high on a tiny sixty-foot-square lot [10].

As a result, even though MIT had made every effort to create adequate laboratory space, the campus by the turn of the century was not only inefficient, but also out of step with contemporary demands for a cohesive collegiate atmosphere, on-site dormitories, sports facilities, libraries, and adequate student unions. Universities like Princeton, Columbia, West Point, Stanford, and Wisconsin had already set a standard in this respect. Designed by the top architectural firms of the nation, they were embedded in park-like environments with plenty of room for expansion. The Carnegie Institute Extension, which had opened in Pittsburgh in 1907, was downright palatial. Furthermore, with the Land Grant Act of 1861, state universities were springing up all across the nation, many with excellent laboratory facilities. At MIT, the decline in student enrollment after 1903 was a direct consequence of the competition from these schools as well as from the new technical universities such as the Illinois Institute of Technology, founded in 1890; the Carnegie Technical Institute (later Carnegie Mellon University), founded in 1900; and the California Polytechnic State University, founded in 1901.[12] To top things off, Harvard University in 1911 had commissioned a cluster of new buildings for their Science Department.[13]

It was not only the general academic environment that was of concern, but also the destinies of two departments in particular, Chemistry and Electrical Engineering. Work in these fields called for a research culture that differed widely from the notion of the sciences that had been adequate in MIT's earlier days. By the end of the nineteenth century these sciences were driven in particular by business considerations and research was increasingly associated with patent generation. It was for this reason that Theodore Newton Vail, the first president of the AT&T Corporation, for example, cultivated a close relationship with MIT and its Electrical Engineering Department. The first generation of his telephone patents were running out, and he was in need of a new generation of more sophisticated patents to maintain the company's competitive advantage. As a consequence, Vail became a substantial benefactor of MIT and served as a member of the visiting committees that periodically reviewed the curriculum of the Electrical Engineering Department.[14] Not surprisingly, it was his library that was in Bosworth's design of 1913 to be housed under the great dome of the projected new building.[15] AT&T's second president, the Bostonian Frederick P. Fish, continued the close and mutually rewarding relationship with MIT. He served on its Executive Committee and was once even asked to become president of MIT. One of the country's leading patent lawyers, he had a hand in some of the most spectacular patent cases of his era, including the patent for Alexander Graham Bell's telephone, the Wright Brothers' 1906 patent for the "flying machine," and the patent for Thomas Edison's light bulbs.

A similar relationship between academic and corporate research was taking place in chemistry. As Fish himself stated, "I should like to prophesy that we are now only at the beginning of this great industrial development and that never will the need for schools such as the Massachusetts Institute of Technology be so great as in the coming years. Chemistry will develop even more wonderfully than has electricity in recent years."[16] He was referring not only to the presence of men closely associated with the chemical industries on MIT's board of trustees,[17] but in particular to the efforts of MIT graduate Thomas Coleman du Pont (1863–1930), who, as president of E. I. du Pont de Nemours Powder Company, had transformed the firm from a family-owned

11

explosives business into a large, centrally managed chemical manufacturing concern.[18] To promote the scientific research his company needed, he had set up an Experimental Station in 1903 near Wilmington, Delaware, filled with MIT graduates. Thomas du Pont, too, became an important benefactor and contributor to MIT.

To address the emerging disciplinary needs of electrical engineering and chemistry, the Research Laboratory in Physical Chemistry and the Research Laboratory in Applied Chemistry were opened in 1903; and the Augustus Lowell Laboratory for Electrical Engineering opened in 1912 **[11, 12]**. The latter was designed by the MIT graduates William P. Rand and Theodore H. Skinner, and was located behind the Pierce Building.[19] In keeping with the imperative to build in a manner as advanced as the teaching itself, the construction engineer

11 Photograph of Augustus Lowell Laboratory for Electrical Engineering, ca. 1910.

12

12 View from Engineering Building "A" looking onto the roof of the Augustus Lowell Laboratory for Electrical Engineering, ca. 1903.

of the Lowell Laboratory was Frank B. Gilbreth (1868–1924), known for his photographic studies of motion and work that foreshadowed the principles that came to be known as scientific management; especially for the MIT laboratory project, he designed a novel concrete-pouring method meant to reduce labor costs.[20]

Despite this hectic building activity, the pace of change was so overwhelming that MIT could not move quickly enough to adapt its older buildings. A drawing of the John Cummings Laboratory of Mining, Engineering, and Metallurgy clearly shows the limitations of that facility **[13]**. Located in the basement of the Rogers Building, the lab was difficult to access, fumes must have been bothersome, and safety was compromised. In the early 1890s, the blast furnace exploded, nearly killing a professor. Fire was also a constant concern, even for MIT's new laboratory buildings. Although the building was constructed of brick and stone on the outside, its support beams and floors

13

were made of wood. Some laboratories had instruments that were too heavy for the floors or were easily affected by the dust and vibrations of the city streets. In fact, until the School of Industrial Sciences was moved into its own building on Trinity Square in 1889, students in the Rogers Building had to tolerate jarring and tremors, and even later, in the new building, large holes had to be chopped into the floors to accommodate engine test equipment.

13 Engraving of the John Cummings Laboratory of Mining, Engineering, and Metallurgy, ca. 1910.

President Maclaurin and the New Site

With pressure mounting to address the need for advanced laboratory space, as well as to solve issues regarding the campus proper, a move to a new site had become imperative.[1] The first call for relocation was made in 1902 by MIT's renowned chemistry professor Arthur Noyes.[2] "It is highly desirable that the Institute remove to another location," he wrote to Henry Smith Pritchett, the president of MIT, adding that he hoped MIT could find a place "where there will be ample room for growth and development, and where the Institute may attain a dignity and collegiate individuality commensurate with its importance and scarcely possible in its present location."[3] The task of deciding where to move to was so daunting, however, that neither Pritchett, who served from 1900 to 1907, nor even Noyes, who served as acting president from 1907 to 1909, could come up with a workable solution. To move the project forward, the faculty had to search outside its ranks for a new president, one who could lead the institution into the new century. In 1901, Frederick P. Fish was approached, but declined.[4] The position was then offered to John R. Freeman, a noted hydraulics engineer, but he, much to his later regret, also turned it down.[5] Finally, Richard Cockburn Maclaurin (1870–1920), a Scottish-born New Zealander, agreed to tackle the problem **[14]**.[6] Educated at Cambridge University, he was at the time teaching physics at Columbia University and was also serving as the chair of the Department of Mathematical Physics. Maclaurin, thirty-nine years old, was inaugurated on June 7, 1909, and it was to be under his guidance that the transformation of the MIT we know today began to take place.

The choice of Maclaurin was not without risk. He knew little about Boston and, for that matter, about MIT. He was, however, a man of enormous energy and an excellent orator, able to put into plain language what, according to him, MIT's vision of itself should be. Unlike President Pritchett, who was aiming for a nuanced balance between the "mechanical" and the "spiritual" aspects of MIT's institutional direction, Maclaurin saw the mission of MIT as revolving around the expanded definition of research.[7] "Some say that we encourage research too much," he wrote in 1911, but "talk of this kind is for the most part nonsense. . . . As we conquer peak after peak, we see regions in front of us full of interest and beauty, but we do not see our goal, we do not see the

14

horizon. In the distance tower still higher peaks which will yield to those who ascend them still wider prospects."[8] The central idea, he argued, is to guide research so that it is "based on training in the art of being useful," with the change that MIT was to undergo, being "the necessary development of the old spirit due to new conditions."[9] And by "new conditions," he meant the "engineering methods and principles [that] are entering more and more into certain branches of business."[10] The great problem of the age is "to organize our knowledge and to organize it in such a way as to make it as effective as possible in industry."[11] MIT's alumni journal, *The Technology Review,* echoed Maclaurin's sentiments, noting that in this "era of business and great business development," MIT appreciates "the necessity for a different sort of education to meet changing conditions in the United States."[12]

Despite Maclaurin's grand aspirations, the fact of the matter was that MIT was in difficult straits. Unlike other universities that had come to rely on donations by business tycoons such as the Rockefellers, Carnegies, Vanderbilts, and Stanfords, MIT, at the time, still considering itself a public institution, had no such sponsor and was continually appealing to the state for extra operating funds. But these were for paltry sums. Harvard University saw in this a buying opportunity. It offered to take over MIT's debts and bring about a merger with its own Lawrence Scientific School. In 1905, the discussions had firmed into an actual proposal under the terms of which MIT would move to a site on the

14 Photographic portrait, Richard Maclaurin, 1912.

Charles River just south of Harvard's new sports stadium. In return, Harvard would discontinue its Lawrence Scientific School. The proposal caused heated debates among students and alumni. Should MIT, after forty years of independence, come under the sway of Harvard? To make the matter even more complex, the site that had been proposed was partially owned by Andrew Carnegie, who, as benefactor of the Carnegie Institute in Pittsburgh, might also expect a quid pro quo in respect to concessions from MIT.[13]

Fortunately, nothing was acted upon and Maclaurin, when he became president, made it clear that "there was to be no more talk of a merger with Harvard."[14] But that meant not only that fundraising would now have to be a top priority of his presidency, but that as a consequence MIT would have to change from a public institution to a private one. To that effect, Maclaurin traveled untiringly throughout the United States, meeting with alumni and exhorting them again and again to step up to the plate for that "supreme effort."[15] Even though many doubted MIT's alumni would meet the challenge, Maclaurin went ahead and set up a committee to seek out potential sites for the new campus. Properties in Chicago and Cleveland were considered as well as dozens of local ones. Some alumni had hoped MIT would move to Springfield, others that it would move further out along Commonwealth Avenue. The site finally chosen was in Cambridge on a flat, fifty-acre field on the Charles River only recently filled in. On one side, the area was delimited by the Charles River Road, now called Memorial Drive [15, 16]. To the west of the site ran the newly created extension of Massachusetts Avenue that led to a new bridge over the Charles River that in turn terminated in a street then called West Chester Park, which marked the terminus of Commonwealth Avenue. Initially, the city of Cambridge had planned the site as a residential quarter, with east-west streets intersected by smaller north-south ones on the model of the Back Bay. But Cambridge had difficulties with that project as few people wanted to live near the factories and tenement houses that were in the immediate neighborhood. Negotiations with Cambridge started in November 1911, and in March 1912, the land was acquired in a deal accelerated by Thomas Coleman du Pont's generous contribution of $500,000 toward the purchase price of $775,000.[16] This was a major triumph for Maclaurin, who promised in exchange that the first building was to be a chemistry research laboratory.[17]

The site, architecturally speaking, was not for the faint of heart. Massachusetts Avenue on both sides of the river had become the address of numerous grand buildings in the classical style. To the north, Harvard University had finished Langdell Hall (1906) with its monumental Ionic façade [17] and was already in the planning stages for Widener Library (completed

15

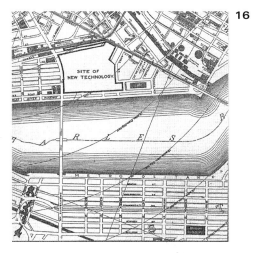

16

15 View south to Boston from Cambridge shore, ca. 1910.
16 Site map of Charles River showing the MIT site, 1912.

in 1915), which was to be a massive Corinthian temple to knowledge. The Cambridge Savings Bank, with grand Ionic columns gracing its Massachusetts Avenue front, was erected in 1904. On the Boston side of Massachusetts Avenue was the new and, for Boston, certainly gigantic extension of the Christian Science Center Church. A block away, Symphony Hall had just been built, which, in turn, was adjoined by the New England Conservatory of Music, both in the monumental Ionic style. Horticultural Hall and the new Boston Opera House were nearby as well. A bit further down on Huntington Avenue was Boston's Museum of Fine Arts building. The monumental Ionic colonnade on its new wing had just been completed in 1911. Also part of Boston's classical landscape, and perhaps one of its finest examples, was the Harvard Medical

17

18

17 Langdell Hall, Harvard
University, Cambridge,
Massachusetts, Shepley,
Rutan and Coolidge, 1906.
18 Harvard Medical School,
Boston, Massachusetts, 1904.

School with its white marble exterior framing a grand open court [18]. The MIT building, regardless of its style, was destined to become an important link in this chain of great neoclassical buildings.

Maclaurin was well aware of the challenge: "We have a glorious site and glorious opportunities, but our task of design is not made more easy by the great expectations of Boston." He was determined that the result should not disappoint.

> If we do not rise to the level of this great [architectural] question we will commit a crime against Technology students for generations to come and a crime against the whole community in which they live and move. . . . What is that impress to be? Will it adequately express the ideals of the Institute, the nobility of its purpose and the dignity of its work? Will those ideals be presented as impressively and as beautifully as by the towers and spires and other architectural features characteristic of the great churches of the Middle Ages? If they do not, it will be a permanent slur on our intelligence and on our taste, for the idea of education for which the Institute stands is as noble an ideal as any that can be expressed by form, and it is pre-eminently the ideal of the thoughtful section of *the* American people today.[18]

No doubt, without that powerful statement of mission the design for MIT would not have been as successful as it was.

The First Design of Stephen Child

MIT had begun to assess its spatial requirements and solicit design proposals even before the Cambridge site had been purchased. One such proposal was published in MIT's *Technology Review* in April 1911 **[19]**. The unsigned drawing might have been the product of the Boston firm of Shepley, Rutan and Coolidge, which had not only completed Frederick Law Olmsted's plan for Stanford University but had also designed the Harvard Law School in Boston.[1] The design featured a domed administration building fronting onto a rectangular lawn, the sides of which were defined by various departmental buildings in Georgian Revival style; the buildings were of brick ornamented with marble around windows and doors. This style had become increasingly popular in the second half of the nineteenth century, ever since the 1876 centennial, and had gained further impetus by the success of the Spanish-American War.[2] Characterizing the architecture of Boston through the first quarter of the twentieth century and later, the Georgian Revival style had already made its

19

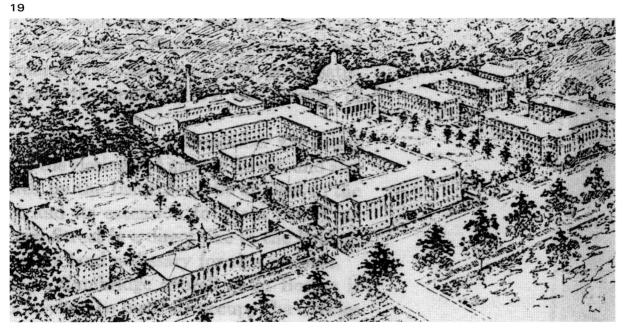

19 A proposed MIT campus, 1911.

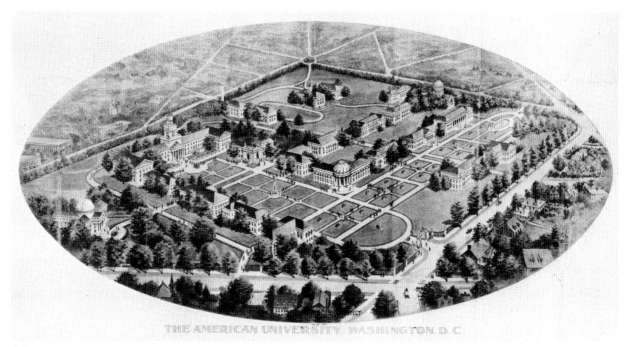

20

impact on Harvard Yard beginning around the turn of the century with the Harvard Union (1902).[3]

One of the most typical examples of this style in the context of a campus is Henry Ives Cobb's 1898 plan for the American University in Washington, D.C., which was, however, never built **[20]**. Cobb, a prominent institutional architect, was also the designer of the master plan of the University of Chicago. The domed end-piece of the American University plan was modeled on the Thomas Jefferson campus in Virginia, even though the side pavilions were significantly more monumental than those of its noted model. Cobb's design, much like this unsigned design for MIT, inclined toward the rhetorical grandeur of a statehouse complex.

Although the unsigned scheme for MIT did not get accepted, it served as the starting point for the first official proposal, which was submitted on December 30, 1911, just four days after the city of Cambridge had agreed to go forward with the sale of the building site to MIT **[21, 22]**.[4] The designer of this first proposal, Stephen Child (1866–1936), had graduated from MIT in 1888 with a major in civil engineering. From 1891 to 1901 he had been deputy street commissioner and superintendent of the sewer department of the city of Newton, Massachusetts; from 1901 to 1903 he had studied at Harvard University under Olmsted, subsequently establishing himself as a specialist in city and landscape planning, in which capacity he had designed several parks

20 Drawing of the unbuilt American University in Washington, D.C., Henry Ives Cobb, 1898.

21

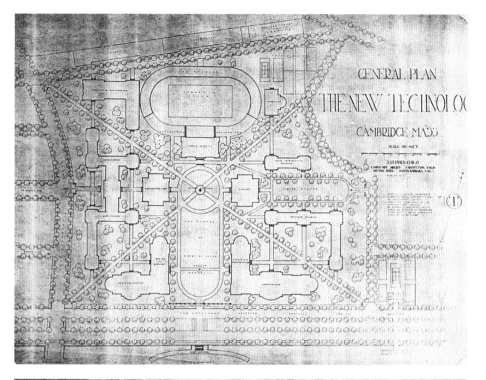

22

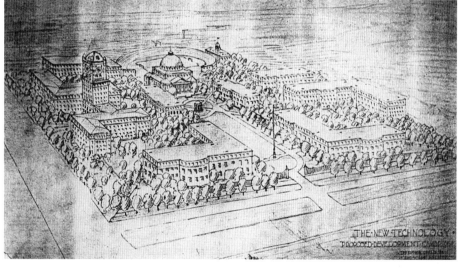

21 Plan of a proposed MIT campus, Stephen Child, 1911.
22 Drawing of a proposed MIT campus, Stephen Child, 1911.

in California from his offices in San Francisco.[5] Although Child had very little experience in campus design, his background as an MIT alumnus and his association with Olmsted seemed to qualify him as a candidate for the commission. His design called for a group of more or less generic Georgian-styled, brick-clad, L-shaped buildings loosely arranged around a free-standing, domed memorial building. The dominant theme of his layout was a large X-shaped circulation system positioned so that one of the avenues ran from the corner

23

of Massachusetts Avenue and Vassar Street pointing directly toward the Massachusetts State House across the Charles River, as if paying homage to that institution. To the north of the site was a large sports field with a dormitory, and there was a gate-tower along Massachusetts Avenue.

At first glance, the design seemed to have given MIT just about everything it wanted: a prominent central building, a sports field, and a quiet, park-like atmosphere. On closer inspection, however, the plan had serious drawbacks that revealed Child's inexperience in campus architecture. The buildings were in a variety of shapes and sizes, with one even butting against the curve of the stadium. The frontage of the campus along the Charles River was left unstudied and a fence actually separated the campus from the river. Child apparently had borrowed this idea from Harvard University, where fences and gates had recently been installed to protect its perimeter. For the MIT location this fence was entirely inappropriate as it separated the campus from the advantage of its river frontage. The only architectural flourish was at the crossing of the paths in the form of a small memorial to MIT's third president, General Francis Amasa Walker, modeled, charmingly but incongruously, on the Temple of Love at the Petit Trianon in Versailles.

The most vociferous criticism of the proposal at the time came from the committee that had been set up to define the parameters of the planned Walker Memorial building and administer the funds laid by for the purpose of a student union. The committee loudly protested the location of the sports stadium at the far side of the grounds. They preferred that the stadium and the Walker building be placed right next to Massachusetts Avenue [23].

23 View of a proposed sports field along Massachusetts Avenue, 1912.

Désiré Despradelle's Alternative

The inadequacies of Child's plan became painfully evident when compared with the plans submitted by Constant Désiré Despradelle (1862–1912), then a professor at MIT, who had been given the green light to make a counterproposal in May 1911 **[24]**. Unlike the U.S.-trained Child, Despradelle had studied at the École des Beaux-Arts in Paris, then the preeminent design school in the world.[1] He had been brought to MIT in 1893 by Francis Ward Chandler, chair of the Department of Architecture, in an effort to build up MIT's reputation as America's leading proponent of Beaux-Arts architecture. In 1898, Despradelle had won third prize in the Phoebe Hearst Competition for a campus design for the University of California at Berkeley, which consisted of rigorously symmetrical buildings around an axis that led from the bottom to the top of a hill. Yet, it still had a relaxed and generous ambiance, largely due to the elongated courts around which the faculty buildings were positioned. Despradelle had

24 Photographic portrait, Désiré Despradelle, 1911.

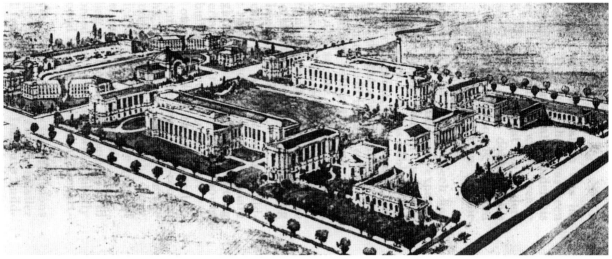

25

also designed several buildings in Boston, including the Berkeley Building (1905), some factory and warehouse buildings at Causeway and North Washington Streets (1906–1912), and the acclaimed Peter Bent Brigham Hospital, now Brigham and Women's Hospital, the central element of which is still standing.[2]

Calling on a faculty member to submit a design may have arisen out of MIT's wish to showcase the competence of its own architectural department, the oldest in the country, which MIT considered, with justification, the strongest as well. Despradelle's initial proposal, drawn from a bird's-eye perspective, shows a small campus on a long and narrow site that is clearly not the Charles River site, which had not yet been bought [25].[3] According to this plan, the campus is divided into three sections: academic, research, and residential. It is laid out axially in the manner of world exhibition grounds, with the administration building and the library at the front and the Walker building in the rear, marking off the entrance to the dormitory complex. That the scheme had the appearance of a world's fair was no accident. The Columbia Exposition of 1893 in Chicago and the Omaha, Buffalo, and St. Louis fairs had set the stage for large-scale plans and grand comprehensive schemes. Despradelle was clearly trying to point MIT in that direction.

It might be useful to compare Despradelle's scheme to the project for the Science laboratories designed by his American-trained contemporary Alexander Wadsworth Longfellow [26]. Although Despradelle was designing a larger set of buildings, the strong symmetry, the interconnected buildings, and the layering of zoning from front to back are similar. What is different is the flow between the buildings: Despradelle conceptualized the campus as a

25 Drawing of campus design for MIT, Désiré Despradelle, 1911.

26

continuum, whereas Longfellow's design, despite its symmetry, is a choppy assemblage of discrete units.

    Despradelle's plan, however, lacked laboratory buildings adequate for MIT's needs. In his next plan, which was probably made in the spring of 1912, Despradelle, now with the building site in mind, shifted the tone completely. We see a single, multi-armed building organized around a central axis that linked a freestanding library at the front to the power plant at the rear **[27]**. Its chimney was not disguised to look like a bell tower, as it was in Longfellow's plan, but is shown in one of the drawings belching steam, symbolizing the modern age. Those departments that needed power from the plant, like the Electrical and Mechanical Engineering Departments, were placed in its proximity around an "Experimental Court," as Despradelle called it, while the Architecture and Physics Departments were located facing the Charles River.

    Subsequently, Despradelle improved his design by widening the Experimental Court, adding two labs for electrical and mechanical engineering, and integrating the library and the auditorium into the fabric of the structure **[28, 29, 30, 31, 32, 33, 34]**. Although the new plan was far superior to

26 Partially executed Science laboratories, Harvard University, Cambridge, Massachusetts, A. W. Longfellow Jr., 1911.

27

28

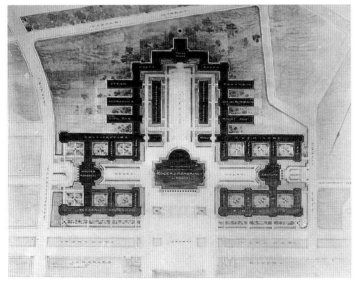

27, 28 Plans of the proposed MIT campus, Désiré Despradelle, 1912.

29

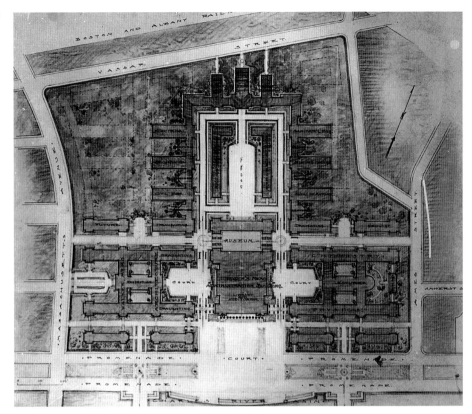

30

29, 30 Plans of the proposed MIT campus, Désiré Despradelle, 1912.

31

32

31, 32 Plans of the proposed MIT campus, Désiré Despradelle, 1912.

33

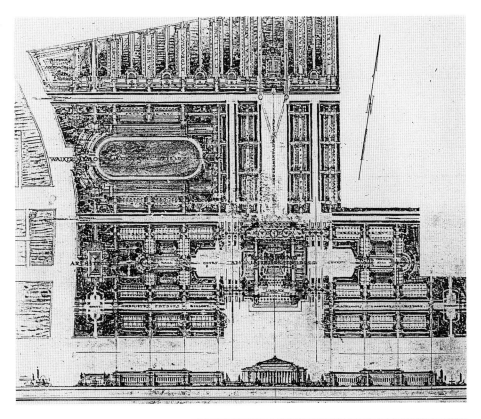

34

33 Final plan and elevation
for the MIT campus, Désiré
Despradelle, 1912.
34 Bird's-eye drawing of the
final version of the proposed
MIT campus, Désiré
Despradelle, 1912.

the first one, it still lacked a dormitory hall and a sports field, a problem which Despradelle addressed in the next set of designs by placing the student housing at the corner of Massachusetts Avenue and Vassar Street around a recreational field. In one version, he closed off the Experimental Court from the academic buildings in front and either removed or internalized the auditorium into the Walker Memorial building. In another scheme that foreshadowed the final version, he integrated all the buildings into a close-knit structure aerated by equally sized rectangular courtyards.

In all these variants Despradelle attempted to integrate the Charles River façade with a Massachusetts Avenue entrance, adding or changing elements as indicated. What is remarkable is that there were no domes. Nineteenth-century civic classicism had made the dome such an important part of its vocabulary that its absence appears to express a shift in Despradelle's design philosophy. If one compares the first and the last drawings it is clear that he went against the grain of the times toward a style more Greek or early Roman in flavor. From a formal point of view, the design had evolved into an almost carpet-like pattern of interwoven rectangles. He added two pedestrian streets that crossed the entire site west to east, dividing the scheme into three horizontal zones. Along Vassar Street, he positioned the larger buildings, such as the gymnasium, to allow for future expansion. The middle zone was dedicated to dormitories and the Experimental Court, while the river zone contained classroom-oriented disciplines like architecture, history, and biology.

A Third Design: Ralph Adams Cram's?

Whereas Child's plan was self-consciously American in tone, with its central "green" and Georgian buildings, Despradelle's was more representative of the ambitions of the Institute and was certainly more expensive. But it had faults as well. The location of the dormitories caused the laboratories and the engineering faculties to be squeezed together. The issue was not resolved even in the last plan, where the labs were placed at the border of the site almost as a sort of industrial backyard. Throughout, Despradelle stressed the formal over the pragmatic. Nonetheless, Despradelle's plan seemed to be generally the more favored. In comparing his plan with that of Child, one commentator wrote the following:

> Nothing more unlike the old-fashioned New England college type could be imagined than this projected array of be-columned, be-domed, and be-porticoed structures facing the pleasant water of the Charles River. . . . It is going to speak in a most insistent tone of the modern trend in education as distinguished from that education which our forefathers knew and planted in the wilderness.[1]

There were, however, other proposals, including an especially fanciful one that placed MIT on an island in the Charles River. This rather bold suggestion had been forwarded by Ralph Adams Cram, who was to become a professor at MIT in 1914 and who already had to his credit designs for Park Avenue Christian Church and the Cathedral of St. John the Divine, both in New York.[2] Furthermore, he also had considerable experience in campus design, Princeton University and West Point being among the crowning achievements of his firm. His interest in an island in the Charles River, most certainly a daring and interesting idea, dates to 1907 when he suggested that an island, modeled loosely on the Île de Cité in Paris, be built to house a cathedral and civic buildings **[35]**.[3] When that project failed to find support, Cram, in 1911, proposed that the island be designed for the MIT campus.[4] The mayor of Boston endorsed the idea and, in fact, incorporated it into the 1911 report of the Joint Board of Metropolitan Improvements, a commission established by the state legislature to consider public works, highways, and issues of civic improvement.[5] The firm of Bellows and Gray drew up several island schemes, one

35

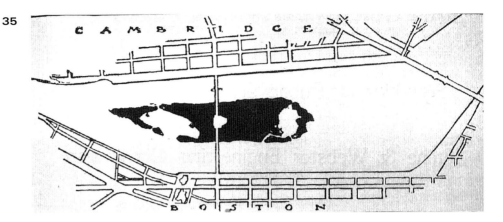

actually with an MIT campus sketched in. The idea had to be abandoned when MIT bought the Cambridge site, even though there was lingering hope that an island, mainly used for recreation, could still be constructed.[6]

This summarizes all of the proposals, but for one anonymous scheme. This project was not signed, and only a single, blurry photograph survives in MIT's archives. It shows buildings in a plain Romanesque style, forming a loose, chain-like wall around the perimeter of the site, leaving a large space in the middle for a park, an open-air Greek theater, and a sports stadium **[36]**. The dorms are along the eastern edge, while the Chemistry building formed the northern terminus. At the bottom of the plan, we see the Charles River façade that consists of horizontally proportioned buildings of various designs and shapes. The only element that marks the campus in the landscape is a solitary tower at the eastern corner. Overall, the campus was apparently meant to appear as if it had grown organically from one or two buildings with add-ons over time.

There are several possibilities as to the originator of this design. Charles Howard Walker, a noted Boston architect and educator in the decorative arts, comes to mind. Walker had designed Boston High School in a very similar stripped-down medieval style. Nor can one rule out the possibility that the submission was made by Ralph Adams Cram, who was a good friend of Walker's. While the style is not in Cram's characteristic neo-Gothic, the linearity of the buildings and the emphasis on the silhouette are not atypical of his style. At any rate, despite the genius of the relaxed and almost proto-functionalist aesthetic of the scheme, there were serious drawbacks, the most important of which was that expansion would be next to impossible without ruining the overall rationale of the project. Furthermore, the façade, when viewed from Boston, was rather prosaic and would not have satisfied MIT's desire for a prominent architectural statement.

35 Site plan showing proposed island in the Charles River, 1911.

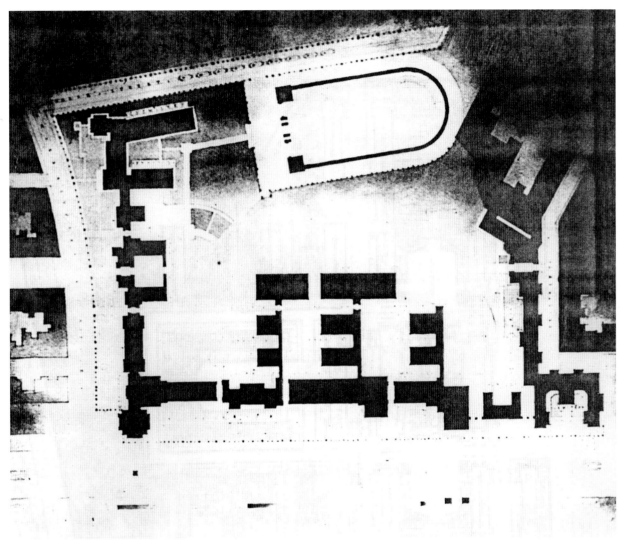

36

36 Unsigned plan of a proposed MIT campus, 1912.

The Eastman Millions

Although the faculty minutes are not preserved, the factional debates must have been lively. Child's plan, with its enclosing wall and punctuating gates, may have appeared too much like an updated version of Harvard Yard, although it might have appealed to those in favor of restraint. Despradelle's scheme in turn might have placed too much emphasis on symbolism at the expense of practicality. The third plan would have found its critics as well. While the various proposals were being solicited, Maclaurin, of course, continued with the time-consuming task of fundraising, but progress was slow, and before long faculty members were grumbling about the cost-saving measures they feared would be imposed on them. All of that changed dramatically on March 5, 1912, when George Eastman, founder of the Eastman Kodak Co., made out a check to MIT for $2.5 million.[1] Maclaurin rushed to New York to meet Eastman and thank him in person. To assign a name of convenience to the donor, Mr. Eastman preferring to remain anonymous, Maclaurin codenamed the generous patron "Mr. Smith." The $2.5 million donation, however, was only the beginning of "Mr. Smith's" generosity: During his lifetime, he was to give MIT about $20 million in gifts and stocks. A plaque in his honor hangs on the wall in Building 6, the Eastman Laboratory Building, and to this day, students rub their fingers along Eastman's nose for good luck before taking their final exams.

The gift was a stunning victory for Maclaurin and is depicted in MIT's yearbook as a goddess spilling her purse of gold coins over the Rogers Building [37]. In a celebratory play composed by MIT students, the following refrain is sung:

> Hurrah! Hurrah! For Tech and Boston's beans, Hurrah! Hurrah!
> For "Smith" who'er that means;
> May he always have a hundred million in his jeans,
> So we'll get—what we want—when we want it.

It was not only that the desired building was now a reality that caused such excitement. Eastman's generosity had put MIT on par with the other major academic institutions that were funded by the great philanthropists of the age.

37

37 Drawing of the Rogers
Building with protectress,
1912.

Freeman to the Rescue

With so much money on hand, many feared MIT might launch recklessly into a building campaign without an orderly planning process. In fact, when Maclaurin announced the successful acquisition of the Cambridge site, he stated somewhat impulsively, and contrary to the plans that had been solicited, that his first priority was a Chemistry building, no doubt to please Thomas Coleman du Pont, who had given half a million dollars for the purchase of the site.[1] The problem was immediately apparent to John Ripley Freeman (1855–1932), a graduate of MIT (1876) and a member of its corporate board **[38]**. Freeman, one of the nation's top civil engineers, had extensive Boston connections. A native of Maine, he specialized in hydraulic engineering and fire prevention and was the president of his own company, the Massachusetts

38

38 Photographic portrait, John R. Freeman.

Mutual Fire Insurance Co. As chief engineer of the 1903 Committee for the Charles River Dam, it was his thorough and extensive study that had persuaded the Massachusetts legislature to go ahead with the dam and the design of the Charles River project.[2] Around 1907, he was offered the MIT presidency, which, to his later regret, he declined.

From the start, Freeman took a keen interest in MIT's design project, and when he heard about Eastman's gift, he wrote a letter to the Executive Committee advising them to resist the temptation "to see the dirt fly."[3] Instead of soliciting design proposals from friends and colleagues and embroiling the institution in protracted turf battles about style, MIT, so he argued, should first conduct a thorough study of its needs. To this effect, he offered his services free of charge.

Thinking this was a reasonable argument and a generous gesture, Maclaurin accepted Freeman's offer, especially since Freeman, from both scientific and practical points of view, was eminently qualified for the task. With the matter, so he felt, in competent hands, Maclaurin stated confidently that MIT would soon have "the most convenient and scientifically designed school of Architecture and Engineering to be found in the world."[4]

Freeman's first step was to reassess the spatial needs of the various faculties. He carefully worked over the numbers that had been presented to him from earlier assessments, expanding Mechanical from 48,000 to 210,000 square feet.[5] Mining, which had originally been slated for 30,000 square feet but then demanded 103,000, was given 87,000.

Once the square footage had been determined, Freeman set out to master the question of design. In this respect he was greatly influenced by the recently published book *Principles of Scientific Management* (1911) by Frederick Winslow Taylor, who in the same year presented his ideas at MIT's yearly alumni banquet.[6] Taylorism, as Taylor's theory soon came to be called, was to become one of the central tenets of American industry; in time it became so generally embraced as to become practically invisible. It swept the country in a popular wave, especially after Henry Ford embraced the method in his automobile manufacturing. Taylor rejected the decentralized production style that was the norm in factories at the turn of the century and argued instead for scientifically organized management that would bring transparency to all levels of production. It was the beginning of the understanding of the role administration could play in the coordination of the production processes, with engineers and managers interacting with practitioners on the factory floor, systematically evaluating problems and options and thereby improving performance.[7] The words "efficiency," "management," and "scientific" were key

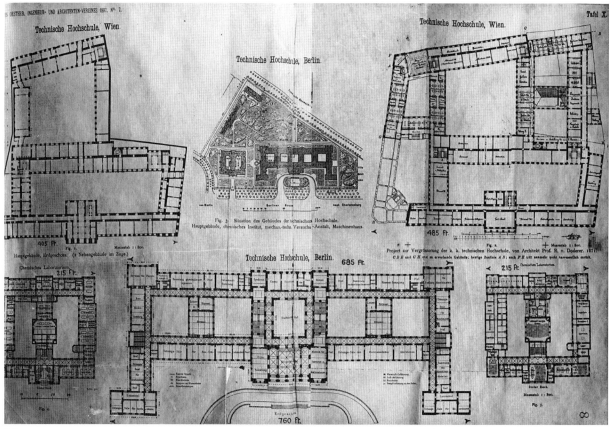

39

39 Comparative plans from "Study No. 7," 1913.

words in the definition of this concept. Freeman, like so many other civil engineers of the time, was an immediate convert and was, in fact, to become a good friend of Taylor's.[8] From that perspective, Freeman saw the architect as an atavism preserved more out of habit than out of need. The architect, he wrote, "is expected by a process [of] half divination, half inspiration, to be able to build with equal authority a public library, a biological laboratory and a pumping station in the monumental style."[9] MIT, he hoped, would avoid this "error" and bring the architect into the game only at the end to provide "suitable and harmonious shells around the internal machinery of the building."[10] The decade before America entered World War I saw extensive professional and popular-press debate over Taylor's theories. From October 1911 until February 1912, a series of hearings in the House of Representatives was held to explore their potential importance in respect to labor legislation. The ideas were particularly popular among engineers and public-sector progressive reformers, as well as among lawyers, ministers, and college administrators.[11]

Freeman apparently never doubted that Maclaurin was on his side in this matter because in his speeches Maclaurin began to employ Taylorist key words,

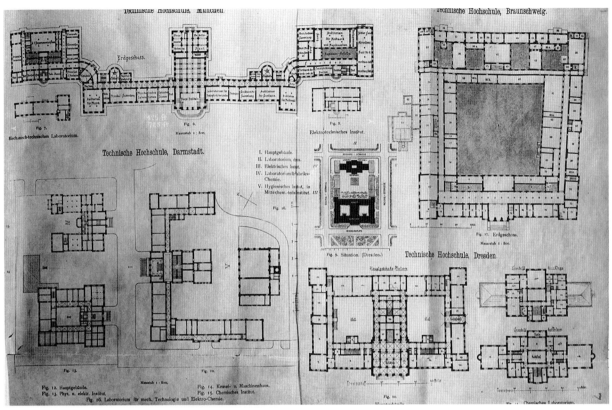

40

40 Comparative plans from "Study No. 7," 1913.

like "scientific," "training," and "efficiency." Indeed, at the same 1911 meeting of the Alumni Association at which Taylor gave his talk, Maclaurin gave a speech on "Educational Efficiency."[12] The great challenge to be faced by MIT, Maclaurin argued, "was to organize our knowledge and to organize it in such a way as to make it as effective as possible in industry."[13] To do this, he held that "Our salvation must come through efficiency and efficiency through training."[14] Maclaurin used these terms, however, only as a way to show that his administration was driven by a singularity of purpose. A closer examination of his notes and comments makes it clear that he was, in fact, disdainful of scientific management being applied to university organizations.[15] Freeman apparently did not see through Maclaurin's rhetoric, which was eventually to lead to a bitter disappointment.

Freeman dove into the project with enormous enthusiasm and energy, collecting and collating material from the various trips he had undertaken in recent years to Mexico, England, and France. He toured the South Kensington Museum, which he much admired. In Paris he registered his pleasure at the Musée des Arts et Métiers, and in Munich, Dresden, and Berlin he viewed the latest scientific departments and laboratory buildings. The Germans, because of generous support from the government, had in that decade become world leaders in many scientific fields, and it was thus natural that he would pay great attention to their design solutions.

To augment his work, Freeman sent out students to make sketches and take photographs; he consulted with construction experts in various fields and corresponded with dozens of specialists, including Albert Kahn, one of the most innovative designers of factories at the time. Freeman also talked with friends and colleagues and collected photographs, postcards, and plans of key buildings. He studied recently built hotels to analyze their designs for corridors and ventilation systems, and he closely examined other buildings to assure himself that the amply dimensioned windows he wanted were compatible with the classical orders. The *Verein Deutscher Ingenieure* sent him information on museums and school buildings in Darmstadt and Berlin.[16] It is obvious that he was already planning beyond a mere assessment of need and functionality and had assumed in his mind the role of designer.

All in all, Freeman created an extraordinarily systematic and exemplary analysis. Over two thousand buildings were studied, with the plans presented on large boards that showed comparisons between the various buildings. A few photographs of the boards still exist in the MIT archives [39, 40]. Had the full documentation survived, it might easily have been the most impressive and complete study of educational buildings ever attempted. All in all, had Freeman's proposal been accepted, the MIT building might have been the first example of a major architectural structure ever erected along Taylorist principles.

"Study No. 7"

In the fall of 1912, with the preliminary version of Freeman's report and analysis available, the Executive Committee could move forward with the process of finding an architect. The logical choice would have been Despradelle, who in May of 1912 was appointed head of the Department of Architecture. But on September 2, 1912, Despradelle suddenly and unexpectedly died—a devastating blow not only to the Department of Architecture, but also to the planning of MIT's campus. On October 14, the Executive Committee met to formally review Despradelle's scheme and to discuss the changed situation. On this occasion Maclaurin indicated in his report to the corporation that despite the excellence of Despradelle's plan, MIT would probably have continued in its search for an architect.[1] Freeman, who had viewed Despradelle's plan with suspicion, seized his opportunity; presuming that his Taylorist design philosophy would sit well with MIT's pro-corporate agenda, he worked feverishly through the winter months, eventually presenting what he called "Study No. 7" to the Executive Committee on January 6, 1913.[2] As it turned out, it was more than just a study of MIT's spatial needs as had originally been agreed upon, but a finished design project introduced by a terse and tightly reasoned explanation of his thinking.

One of the first things Freeman stressed in the presentation was that architects, in his view, preoccupied with aesthetics, rarely thought through the question of use and function. He cited numerous examples, such as the following, with the names of the "guilty" tactfully omitted.

> The professor in charge, when he protested better light was needed than was promised by the plans in rooms where much work of dissection and microscopy was carried on, was told in effect by the architect that,—"what you ask for would upset the whole architectural unity of this campus. Can't you see that it is impossible to have anything other than Tudor-Gothic windows of moderate size in this place?"[3]

Although Freeman was not irrevocably opposed to considerations of style, what he really wanted was a building that, though classical in appearance, was fully efficient in its use. Such a building, he argued, would have to be designed "from the inside out," which meant that the MIT building was to be a

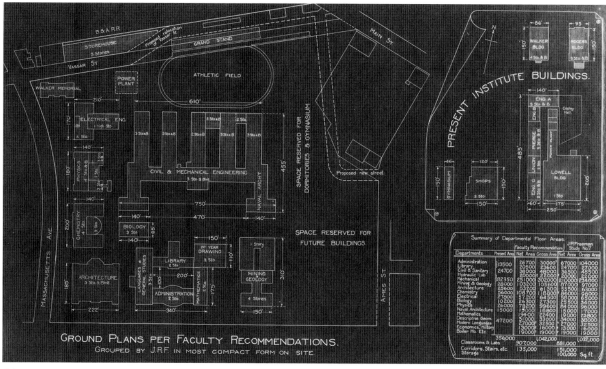

41

building "one-fifth architecture and four-fifths a problem of industrial engi-neering."[4] With pride he declared that such a building would, in the final analysis, be a "glorified factory."[5]

To reinforce this point, MIT would have to reject the "United States model of putting departments into separate buildings" in which the professor in charge of a department "reigns undisturbed, largely in a little kingdom of his own" whereas the students run "much risk of colds in our northern cli-mate, in passing from one lecture to another."[6] In Europe, he argued, one finds departments "housed in a single connected group closely resembling the arrangement of the best modern factories." American universities, he added, were still young and had grown in a piecemeal fashion. Playing devil's advo-cate, Freeman created a plan based on the "American model," using faculty rec-ommendations of the square footage to show how inefficient such a scheme would be when compared to his own suggested plan for a single massive build-ing oriented toward efficiency of space. His American-style plan was, of course, meant to demonstrate how unprogressive such an approach was [41]. It was a brilliant ploy.

Freeman's argument was so convincing that the plan for a Harvard-style campus was abandoned in favor of one massive structure. Even though

41 Plan "based on faculty recommendations," John Freeman, 1913.

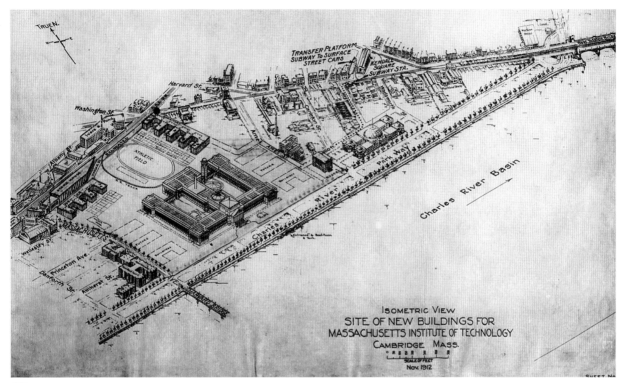

42

42 Isometric view of proposed MIT campus, John Freeman, 1913.

Bosworth was later to take credit for this, it cannot be denied that the initial conception and defense were Freeman's.

The building, close to Charles River Road, would offer frontage to the city and be sited in the middle of the property in the anticipation that subsequent buildings along Massachusetts Avenue would shield it from noise. Dormitories and a sports field were put toward the back and were considered secondary issues by Freeman. The guiding priorities for the building, so Freeman described in his presentation notes, were as follows:

1. A flood of window light
2. Fresh air
3. Avoidance of unnecessary traffic
4. A consideration for the psychology of the students
5. A uniform construction technique

The building's footprint was in the shape of an E laid sideways against Charles River Road [42, 43, 44]. The central element contained all the specialized parts of the program: the administration building, the auditorium, and the power plant. At the far end stood an impressively scaled mechanical and electrical laboratory, Freeman's special pride and joy. The five-story-high

43

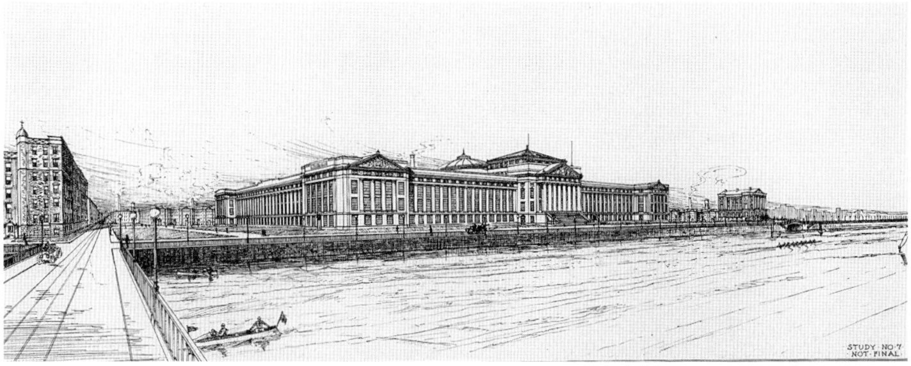

44

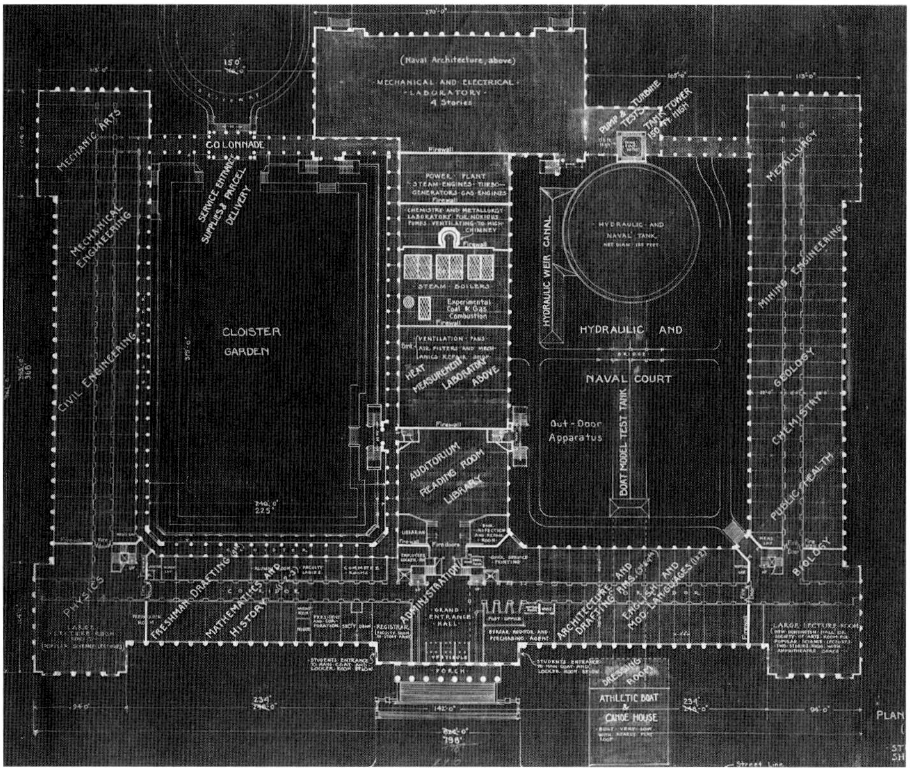

structure, which had no basement, was fronted by a pedimented Doric entrance facing the Charles River **[45, 46]**. One of the courtyards was to contain a state-of-the-art naval engineering laboratory, and the other one, which he called "a cloister," was to have benches on all floors facing toward the space where students and faculty could meet and rest between classes, accommodating a thousand people at a time **[47]**. The last category, "a uniform construction technique," spoken like a true civil engineer, was aimed to lessen the cost of a building of one million square feet. It came with the proposal for a

43 Perspective view from the Harvard Bridge of the proposed academic building, John Freeman, 1913.
44 Plan of the proposed MIT building, John Freeman, 1913.

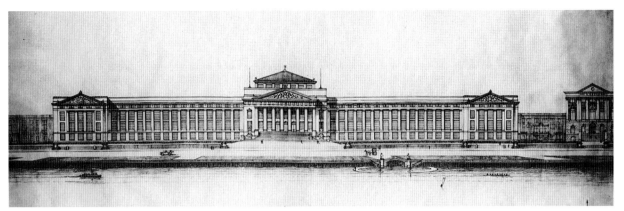

45

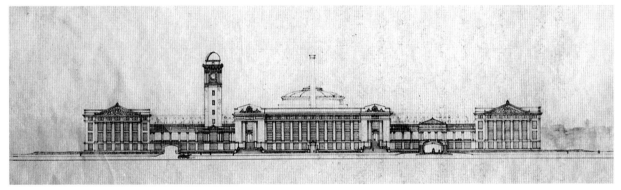

46

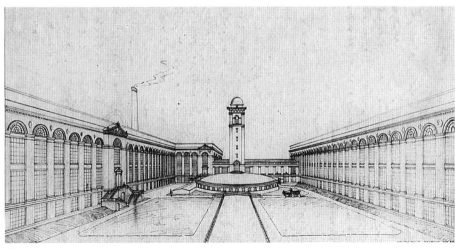

47

45 Front elevation of the
proposed MIT building, John
Freeman, 1913.
46 Rear elevation of the
proposed MIT building, John
Freeman, 1913.
47 View into Naval and
Hydraulic Court, John
Freeman, 1913.

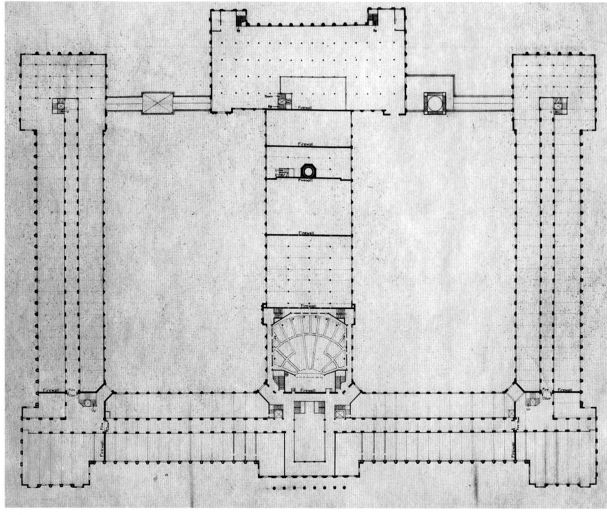

48

48 Structural plan of the proposed MIT building, John Freeman, 1913.

concrete frame with supporting column pairs running down the center. Rooms were to be created by means of "curtain walls," as he phrased it, consisting of lightweight material that could be built up or removed to make classrooms or offices as needed **[48]**.

The use of reinforced concrete was highly unusual and went against the professional norm. Albert Carman, a physics professor, researching the specifications for a laboratory for the University of Illinois, recommended the use of extra-heavy masonry with many stabilizing cross walls running the full height of the building in order to reduce vibrations.[7] Requiring substantial foundations, this approach was rejected by Freeman. Reinforced concrete would weigh less—an important point, since the building was constructed on landfill—but would allow both broad windows and flexible interiors.

49

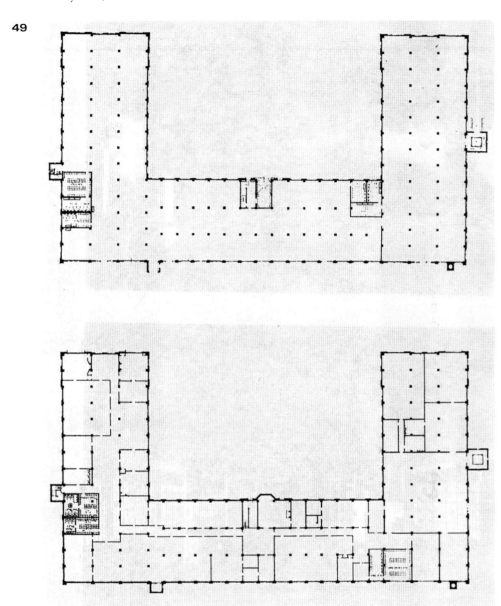

49 Structural plan of the
Country Life Press factory,
Garden City, Long Island,
1911.

Although reinforced concrete is commonly used today, this was not the
case in the early twentieth century when it was used primarily for dams,
bridges, and factories. It was more expensive than steel, but it was fireproof
and allowed for better illumination than conventional brick pier construction.
The reinforced concrete frame consisting of columns holding up floor slabs
had been perfected by Albert Kahn when the Ford factories in Michigan had
been built.[8] The internal arrangement of the column pairs used by Freeman
seems, in fact, to have been derived from Kahn's Dodge Factory in Detroit,

Michigan, but another example is the Country Life Press factory in Garden City, Long Island, both completed in 1911 **[49]**.⁹ A building close to Boston that Freeman would certainly have known was the United Shoe Machinery Company in Beverly, Massachusetts, designed by Ernest L. Ransome in 1903. This particular building would also have pleased Freeman because of its vast expanses of windows. Such buildings were, in fact, described in the trade magazines of the time as "daylight factories" on the assumption that illumination was "one of the few basic essentials to high manufacturing efficiency."¹⁰ Much as "the pure, clear, uncolored daylight" and "the sunshine of roofless fields" had contributed to the rare artisanship of Japanese, Indian, and Italian handworkers, ideal light conditions were now "becoming a possession of the American factory laborer as well."¹¹ In tapping into this new construction technology for an educational building, Freeman was definitely an innovator.

On the exterior of the MIT building, Freeman proposed columns made of artificial stone, a relatively new technology at the time that used a special concrete mix poured into molds. The method was not inexpensive, but Freeman was convinced that it was the wave of the future as it put greater control into the hands of the engineers. Tile was also to be used, and it had the advantage, he pointed out, of being easy to clean, which was no small consideration, since buildings were quickly blackened by coal smoke belching forth from millions of chimneys in the city. The stylistic model for the tile that he envisioned was similar to the Metropolitan Life Insurance building in San Francisco that he so much admired—more for the technology associated with replicating ornate classical details in tiles rather than for the architecture itself. As for stylistic concessions, Freeman chose Doric, with its traditional masculine attributes. In keeping with his desire to bring as much light into the building as possible, the first floor, which would traditionally have been a solid-looking socle, or a foundation zone with small windows, was illuminated by windows that were just as large as those of the floors above. To a classically trained architect, this would have been unacceptable for it makes the Doric pilasters seem to float precariously on the surface of the façade. To give the building a suitable historical garb, however, Freeman modeled the building's main octo-style entrance on the Parthenon in Athens, and in the tympanum he even visualized statues showing the various arts.

Selection of Cass Gilbert

Freeman realized that getting approval for his scheme would be an uphill battle. "I don't know how much longer the Executive Committee will be content to let a mere engineer, to whom things must be efficient before they can be beautiful, in large measure monopolize work which the public regards as the special province of the architect."[1] To garner support, he wrote an article in the *Technology Review* in which he stated that the MIT building was designed "to the satisfaction of the men who are to use this big educational apparatus before ever the architects begin to drape these skeletons with the flesh of pilaster and entablature. . . . This is decidedly the reverse of erecting an ornamental outside shell and cramming the contexts more or less congestedly into it."[2]

On January 17, 1913, Freeman was allowed to present his proposals to the assembly of alumni gathered in New York City, one of the largest alumni gatherings ever.[3] But it was clear from Maclaurin's own presentation at the meeting that things were not going Freeman's way. In tactfully phrased words, Maclaurin made it clear that Freeman's proposal, despite the praise given to it, would be turned down:

> We are warned that the architects are more likely to give us beauty than utility and many horrible examples of inefficient buildings are placed before us for our edification. I believe, however, that the implied criticism of the architect is unjust. The fault is just as likely to be with the client as with the architect. . . . Here we had the great advantage of Mr. Freeman's cooperation and we cannot easily overestimate the great obligation under which he has placed the Institute by his self-sacrificing devotion to the solution of the problem.[4]

And so it was. At the next meeting of the Executive Committee, Freeman's proposal was politely reviewed and rejected, and the choice fell on Cass Gilbert (1859–1934), who had just then finished the Woolworth Building in New York City (1910–1913), a work that had elevated him overnight into the ranks of America's foremost architects [50]. Gilbert, who had in 1907 been elected president of the American Institute of Architects, befriended such political giants as Theodore Roosevelt, William Howard Taft, and others, and his works included

50

such highly visible structures as public libraries, city halls, state capitols, and warehouses. Nor was Gilbert unknown in Boston, where he had designed, among other buildings, the Suffolk Savings Bank in 1905.[5] Most fortuitous for him, however, was that as a graduate of MIT (1880) he had a good insider friend in the person of James Knox Taylor, who had just been appointed head of MIT's Department of Architecture after Despradelle's death. Taylor, who had previously served as a design partner in Gilbert's firm, had been the supervising architect of the United States Treasury Building, another prominent commission executed by Gilbert's firm. We may safely assume that it was Taylor who had championed Gilbert. Gilbert was introduced to Maclaurin on June 13, 1912, at the Tech Club Dinner in New York City, during which Gilbert was one of the featured speakers. No doubt Maclaurin also wanted to congratulate Gilbert on being elected a term member of the MIT corporation.[6] Gilbert was an immensely desirable choice, not least because he also had a good deal of experience with campus design, receiving in 1905 the campus commission for Oberlin College; in 1912 he was named Oberlin's campus architect. Besides Oberlin, Gilbert had also drawn up a plan in 1908 for the University of Minnesota in Minneapolis.

It was soon reported back to the Executive Committee, however, that a satisfactory agreement with Gilbert could not be arranged. Apparently Gilbert chafed under the notion of having to cooperate with Freeman. "I do not regret having taken the stand that I did," he wrote later, adding:

50 Photographic portrait, Cass Gilbert, ca. 1912.

> If Dr. Maclaurin had kept his original proposition of placing the entire work in my hands, I should have done my best to make it a great success; but when they kept narrowing [it] down, I felt that the situation was becoming impossible.[7]

Though there is no further explanation why Gilbert turned down the invitation, one can easily surmise from the actions of the Executive Committee that Gilbert had refused to take on a project that, in essence, already had Freeman's footprint on it. In fact, Freeman was still eagerly at work on developing the details of his scheme. As late as January 24, 1913, a letter from the noted engineer Albert Kahn arrived for Freeman promising to send the requested drawings of factory buildings.[8] Clearly, the situation had to be clarified. On January 27, just after hearing of Gilbert's refusal to even consider the project, the Executive Committee was forced to take an unequivocal stand and get back in the driver's seat. A terse resolution, aimed directly at Freeman, stated the following:

> The time has arrived for placing the whole matter in the hands of the architect, and that Mr. Freeman should not be invited at this stage to proceed further with the study of details.[9]

But Freeman was not so easily dispatched. On February 5, he sent a telegram to Maclaurin proposing that if MIT were to give him the project, he would finish the design for one half of the regular architectural fee and possibly for "even one third."[10] He also promised to have the building completed by the fall of 1913. To summon support, he got a noted alumnus of MIT, Frederick Haynes Newell, then the director of the U.S. Geological Survey, to write a letter that defended his proposal to Freeman's good friend Charles A. Stone, a member of the Executive Committee and one of the leading engineers in the United States.[11] The gauntlet had been thrown down.

William Welles Bosworth Becomes a Candidate

From Maclaurin's perspective, the situation was now desperate. The first designer, Despradelle, had died; Gilbert had not even bothered to consider the project; and Freeman, despite the Executive Committee's warnings, was continuing to agitate from the sidelines. His offer to work on a reduced commission verged on the unprofessional. Furthermore, if Freeman kept soliciting letters on his behalf from the very same alumni that Maclaurin had cultivated for years, Maclaurin could easily fear a public relations crisis. Freeman's offer to work at a reduced fee was almost guaranteed to gain him a measure of support. In order not to lose control of the process, Maclaurin decided to conduct the search from behind closed doors and, because the problem had arisen in the first place out of financial restrictions, he decided once more to turn for help to the great barons of American commerce and industry. It was a brilliant tactical move, since these men were, as Maclaurin knew, not stingy with their financial support—especially if it was ostensibly for a good cause, the support of which might also further their own ambitions.

Among those he contacted was John D. Rockefeller Jr. (1874–1960), who had in 1911 just taken control of the family fortune. Unlike his father, Rockefeller Jr. was not contaminated by the scandals that had swirled around the Standard Oil Co. His interest lay in philanthropy. Indeed, he was to create one of the largest philanthropic organizations ever: the Rockefeller Foundation. One of his many charitable projects included participation in acquiring the grounds for the United Nations Building in New York and beyond that he founded the colonial Williamsburg, Virginia, preservation project, to name just a few of his interests. His father had also been a generous donor, funding, for example, the University of Chicago, but the son put a more cosmopolitan glow on the family image, and his personal architect, William Welles Bosworth (1869–1966), was an important element in that strategy. The two had established ties around 1907, and Bosworth's career remained linked to the Rockefeller name from that time on. At the time, he had just finished the Rockefeller townhouse at 10 West 54th Street and also had recently redesigned Rockefeller's estate north of Tarrytown, the famous Kykuit, where he had transformed a bleak and treeless farm landscape into one of the most spectacular gardens of the period, with its terraces, walks, and exotic plantings **[51, 52]**.[1] Bosworth was also

51

52

responsible to some degree for the architectural expression of the Kykuit
building, working closely with the architects William A. Delano and Chester H.
Aldrich and the interior designer Ogden Codman.[2]

In turning to Rockefeller at this fortuitous time, Maclaurin changed the
entire tone of the MIT commission. It was no longer simply a question of
adding another layer of financial backers, but it brought with it an entirely different set of assumptions that Maclaurin may not actually have anticipated.
Instead of architecture being relegated to a last-minute, grudging concession,
as was the case with Freeman's plan, it had suddenly become a primary consideration, subject to comprehensive planning. Furthermore, unlike Gilbert, who
had declined because of Freeman's interference, Bosworth, who had been suggested by Rockefeller, was used to working for clients with strong personal
convictions. He was flexible and accommodative without, however, making
concessions on the overall vision of a project that was to bear his name.
Particularly fortuitous was the circumstance that Bosworth was actually an
MIT graduate, which removed any latent resistances that might otherwise
have arisen.

51 Façade of Kykuit,
Pocantico Hills.
52 Rear garden of Kykuit,
Pocantico Hills.

11

Bosworth's Early Architectural Training

If Bosworth is not as well known in the United States as other Beaux-Arts architects of that time, it is because his career, under the auspices of Rockefeller Jr., led him to France in the 1920s, where he was put in charge of the restoration of the Palace of Versailles and the Cathedral of Rheims, projects Rockefeller was interested in and that he generously financed. In time, Bosworth was awarded the French Legion of Honor and the French Cross of the Commander of the Order of Arts and Letters, one of the few Americans ever to receive such honors.

Born in Marietta, Ohio, to one of the area's leading families, Bosworth had received his degree in architecture at MIT in 1889.[1] Initially, his design approach was close to the neo-medievalist and arts-and-crafts style that was so well-liked in Boston at the time.[2] It was only in the mid-1890s, when he had moved to New York, that he "converted" to classicism. The ground for that conversion had, however, already been prepared by Bosworth's favorite MIT professor, William Rotch Ware, with whom he had traveled through Europe after his graduation in 1889. Ware was the editor of one of the prominent journals of the time, the *American Architect,* and author of a handbook on neoclassical principles, entitled *American Vignola.* Ware published photos of Bosworth's work in various issues of the *American Architect* and, in 1922, published a feature article on him. Furthermore, he published some of Bosworth's drawings, such as the Rue du Château Josselin in Paris (1889) and one of a garden pavilion, both demonstrating a deft perception and loose, sensitive touch [53]. Today, certain views of the MIT building still reflect that same painterly quality that he had displayed in his drawings and that gave a certain mellowness to all his designs. Later articles featured some of his sketches and observations of buildings and farms from France.

One of Bosworth's first commissions (1889) was for two buildings for the Hampton Normal and Agricultural Institute in Virginia.[3] The school had been established in 1868 for the education of freed slaves and had grown rapidly, with the expansion largely paid for by the trustees, most of whom were East Coast philanthropists and ministers. Bosworth, coming from a line of preachers himself, circulated easily in this environment and, in 1894, married the daughter of Rev. Herbert Lewis Newton, a scholarly and broad-minded liberal

53

53 "Rue du Château Josselin," William Welles Bosworth, 1889.

Episcopal. No doubt he had met the Newton family and his future wife through his principal New York contact, William Reed Huntington, the cousin of his father.[4] Huntington, a leading figure in the Episcopal Church, was rector of Grace Church at Broadway and Tenth Street. (The pulpit in that church, by the way, was designed by Bosworth in 1892.)

In 1896, Bosworth left for Paris to study at the famous École des Beaux-Arts. First, however, he traveled to London, where he devoted several months to the study of classical architecture at the British Museum. There he met and befriended Lawrence Alma Tadema (1836–1912), a Dutch-born painter much admired at that time for his realistic depictions of classical antiquity. Tadema also had a strong following in the United States, with Cass Gilbert and others numbering among his admirers. In his various autobiographical essays, Bosworth points to the significance of his relationship with Tadema. When in the 1920s he had the opportunity to design his own studio in New York at 527 Fifth Avenue, he quoted Tadema's studio windows as his homage to Tadema, adding the Greek words for "healthy life, joy, peace, goodness, and hope," combining his admiration for Tadema with his admiration for all things Greek [54].[5] Furthermore, imitating Tadema's idea of incorporating the letter T in the window, Bosworth designed the top register of his studio around the letter B. Tadema insisted on strict accuracy of measurements, which he personally reaffirmed by visits to archaeological sites in Italy and Greece, a discrimination that impressed Bosworth and that he made his own as well. Staying abreast of the latest archaeological developments, he incorporated elements of Halicarnassus, the Pantheon, the Villa Madama, and Roman temples in his later buildings.

Moving on to Paris, Bosworth was well aware that Tadema's restrained and temperate classicism was not typical for the École, which, at that time, tended toward a more flamboyant architectural expression. Nevertheless, attending the École was certainly a must for anyone who wanted to make a name for himself in the United States, especially during the years following the World Columbian Exposition of 1893 in Chicago. The brand of classicism advocated by the Beaux-Arts school played well with the emerging civic and institutional consciousness of the country, and both Richard Morris Hunt and H. H. Richardson before him had studied at the École between 1843 and 1855. Bosworth thus belonged to a "second generation" of American Beaux-Arts architects that included Ernst Flagg, Charles McKim, John Merven Carrère, and John Russell Pope, all of whom played important roles in the American architectural scene of the first decade of the twentieth century.[6] While in Paris, Bosworth, as was the custom, worked in the ateliers of various designers, including those of Richard Chaussemiche, winner of the 1890 Prix de Rome and official architect for the City of Paris, and Gaston Redon, another Prix de Rome winner, who was in charge of the buildings and restorations of the Louvre.

Upon his return to the United States in 1900, Bosworth worked for the firm Carrère & Hastings, which in 1905 was to make a national name for itself with the design of the New York Public Library. In 1901, under the auspices of the firm, Bosworth was sent to Buffalo, New York, to help in the design realization of the Pan American Exhibition.[7] He was eventually promoted to resident

54

architect of the exhibition and made responsible for the general layout.[8] With its broad inverted T-shaped central court, it was a forerunner of Bosworth's design for MIT. While still at Carrère & Hastings, Bosworth assisted in the design coordination of several buildings at the 1904 Louisiana Purchase Exposition in St. Louis. He also cooperated with the city of Cleveland in developing their plans for urban improvements. During this time, Bosworth was invited to join the Society of Beaux-Arts Architects, which had been set up in 1893 to promote Beaux-Arts aesthetics in academe and practice, and of which he became secretary in 1909.[9]

54 Bosworth's studio, ca. 1920.

Vanderlip, Vail, and Bosworth

While Bosworth was in Buffalo, his first client was John G. Milburn, a noted lawyer and important figure in that town, for whom he designed a summer home in Manhasset, New York.[1] Most of Bosworth's early clients, however, were heavily involved in philanthropy, and it was through that social network that Bosworth began to navigate. One of his early clients in that respect was Richard Jackson Barker (b. 1849), a member of Congress from Rhode Island and a prominent figure in the area who made his money in a lumber business he inherited from his father.[2] Barker's wife, Eliza Harris Lawton, was involved in numerous philanthropic organizations, such as the Rhode Island Sanitary Relief Association and the Tiverton branch of the Rhode Island Anti-Tuberculosis Society, among others. Bosworth designed for the Barkers a garden with a circular temple on the property of their Tiverton, Rhode Island, estate.[3] It was through clients such as these that Bosworth got the commission to design the New York Magdalen Benevolent Society Asylum in New York City in 1904.[4]

Bosworth's career picked up steam when in 1906 he was called in to design a garden for another prominent philanthropist, the New Yorker Valentine Everit Macy, who lived at Scarborough-on-Hudson.[5] This led not only to Bosworth's acquaintance with Rockefeller but ultimately with Frank Vanderlip (1864–1937), both of whom lived near Scarborough-on-Hudson. Vanderlip was president of the City Bank of New York, the most powerful of the banks at that time, a close friend of John D. Rockefeller, and former assistant secretary of the Treasury under President McKinley. Vanderlip's wife was particularly active in the women's suffrage movement in issues relating to mental health.

Although Bosworth's first commission from Vanderlip was relatively modest—a gate for Vanderlip's family estate north of Tarrytown, New York, and some landscaping—he was then commissioned to design a schoolhouse not far from Vanderlip's estate for the children in that exclusive residential area.[6] The building, near the Albany Post Road (now Route 9), still exists today, although it is no longer a school [55].[7] Rectangular in shape, it had a corridor running down the center of the classroom wing, permitting the classrooms to be lined up along both outer walls so that they would receive as much natural light as possible. The corridor itself was illuminated by a clerestory that rose

55

56

above the surrounding roof but was concealed from the front by a rather high
façade parapet. Even today, when you enter the building, the atmosphere of
quiet luminosity is a pleasant surprise **[56]**. The façade, without the traditional
portico of that time, had columns *in antis* and an entablature between the
entrance below and a loggia above. Doric columns, modeled on the Parthenon,
were deployed below, and elegant Ionic ones above. On the whole, the balance
between horizontals and verticals, between solids and voids, imparts a stately
yet modern aspect to the composition. In all likelihood, the underlying model
Bosworth had in mind in designing the façade may have been Andrea
Palladio's Villa Cornaro.

   At about the same time, Vanderlip was appointed to the board of
Letchworth Village, an institution for epileptics and the mentally ill founded in
1907. It was located across the Hudson from Scarborough on a hill not far
from the current town of West Haverstraw.[8] The institution, based on the then

57

58

progressive notion that working with nature had a beneficial effect on mental health, was to be laid out as a working farm. Vanderlip brought in Bosworth to make the plan—a commission that turned into a considerable project. By the time of its completion, the Village consisted of over 100 buildings, including workshops, schools, gymnasiums, and dining halls. The young, middle-aged, and elderly were separated by gender into six zones, with an added zone for administration. The siting was generous, with each area being designed around a different organizational principle, some more compact than others.

The dorms were mostly one-story structures to avoid the difficulty stairs might pose for those with physical disabilities. Most of the buildings, many of which still survive, were T-shaped with central octagonal rooms that led to the wards on the sides and workshops in the middle **[57]**. Built of local fieldstone, they were, so explained Bosworth, "harmonious in that environment," and their modest porticoes painted white in a Jeffersonian style "would never become distasteful with changes of style in years to come."[9]

57 Dormitory building, Letchworth, New York.
58 Photographic portrait, Theodore Newton Vail.

59

The part that was built first was laid out around a long and narrow central green with dining facilities at the ends. A power plant just below the green provided energy for heating and workshops. The school for that particular group, called the Vanderlip Building, was at the cross-axis of the green and had a tall, porticoed entrance and a sizeable auditorium, its wings containing generously proportioned classrooms. Thanks to the quality of the workmanship, most of these buildings survive to this day, even though they are no longer used for their original purposes.

Around 1911, either Rockefeller or Vanderlip recommended Bosworth to Theodore Newton Vail (1845–1920) [58], who promptly gave Bosworth the largest and most visible commission yet: the corporate headquarters of AT&T [59, 60]. It was to be located on a prestigious site in downtown New York City, just a few blocks from Wall Street.[10] Like Bosworth, Vail was from Ohio, although he had grown up in Morristown, New Jersey. He had worked himself up through the ranks of Graham Bell's telephone company, where he had

60

organized a system for financing in order to unify the burgeoning telephone industry. In 1901 Vail left his post at the helm of the company, but he returned in 1907 while also serving as president of the National City Bank of Troy.

The significance of Vail's help to get Bosworth the MIT commission should not be underestimated. Vail had several contacts with MIT, serving periodically on its Visiting Committee and, more importantly, on various Special Committees, such as the one dealing with choosing the site for MIT's new building and with selecting the engineer for the planned new building. There is little doubt that Vail, who announced that he would bequeath his extremely valuable library to the Institute in the same month Bosworth was chosen architect, used his considerable influence to Bosworth's advantage.

Although the AT&T building was incomplete in 1912, Maclaurin would have seen on the plans a modern steel structure clad top to bottom in a Greek-styled exterior, the three-story-high Ionic columns of Vermont granite forming

60 Exterior of AT&T.

61

eight registers over a Doric base. According to Bosworth, the choice of the classical style conformed to Vail's notion of a universal company that wanted to convey a recognizable iconographic presence in all regions and economies. An anonymous *American Architect* article (strongly suspected to have been written by Bosworth) stated that if any style "has the right to our allegiance, it is the Graeco-Roman, the origin of our early American tradition."[11] Not only was the style "likely to outlive all the others," but it was "found from Salem to Salt Lake

61 Lobby of AT&T.

62

City, from Portland to Savannah—in every type of structure; from wharf-houses, customs houses, jails and court houses, to churches and private residences, both in the cities and the country."[12] The lobby of the AT&T building was one of the most unusual ones of the era [61]. Instead of a large double-high space, similar to the nearby Woolworth Building, Bosworth designed a "hypostyle hall" with full-bodied Doric columns modeled on the Parthenon, marking out a grid. Bosworth was seeking to coordinate the classical tradition with the requirements of a modern building. Columns were not merely the decorative elements they had become in the hands of other architects but created all the illusion of being real supports. For the façade Bosworth turned to a structure built during the reign of Septimus Severus (A.D. 193–211) on the flank of the Capitoline Hill. It had, so archaeologists suggested at the time, seven succeeding orders of columns and, as Bosworth himself pointed out, "was considered one of the seven wonders of the world."[13]

It should be noted that when Bosworth was designing the MIT building, he specified that the entrance doors be modeled on those of the AT&T building, no doubt as a subtle homage to Vail, the man most principally involved in getting him the commission [62].

62 Entrance to MIT's Building 10, William Welles Bosworth, 1916.

Bosworth Gets the Nod

On January 17, 1913, when Maclaurin was in New York to speak at the annual meeting of the MIT alumni, he met Bosworth, who personally guided him through the Rockefeller house.[1] Maclaurin was impressed and, perhaps anticipating problems with Gilbert, asked Bosworth to immediately send him information about his design practice. The next meeting of the Executive Committee was on February 17, by the end of which, with Freeman now officially sidelined, Bosworth got the job, with recommendation letters having been hastily assembled from Bosworth's three famous patrons, Rockefeller Jr., Vanderlip, and Vail.[2] It was an impressive and persuasive list. Vail praised the design of the AT&T building, especially its "grand simplicity." Rockefeller wrote that he "was closely associated with Bosworth over the last five or six years" and that all who had visited the gardens of his estate "shared with us the belief that they are exceptionally beautiful not only in general plan, but in every smallest detail." Bosworth, he added, was a man of "unfailing courtesy," who does not work along "stereotyped lines" and was never dogmatic in his opinions.

> I think that one can safely say that Mr. Bosworth has a strong leaning towards simplicity and dignity in architecture rather than complication and ornateness. . . . He never uses ornamentation except with some definite purpose in mind, and then sparingly.[3]

Vanderlip's recommendation emphasized similar points and noted that Bosworth "is a very broad gauged man whose work is always in good taste." To thank Vanderlip for his assistance in resolving the building crisis, MIT elected him life member of the Corporate Board.[4]

On the day Bosworth received the commission, Maclaurin suggested that he write a conciliatory note to Freeman, which Bosworth immediately did:

> Dear Mr. Freeman, Doctor Maclaurin and I have just signed an agreement, and I wish in undertaking this work, to say to you that whoever did it would be under very great obligation to you, for [the] exhaustive way in which you have prepared the ground. I have been greatly impressed with . . . your report and shall no doubt find more and more to respect in it as I study it further. Hoping that I may have the pleasure of meeting you at no distant date to talk over the New Technology, Sincerely, William W. Bosworth.[5]

On that very day, Maclaurin also wrote a letter to Freeman, informing him that research funds for "Study No. 7" had been terminated.[6] Feeling that his hard work was being overlooked, Freeman complained to his friends that he was the "victim of conflicting emotions." Having been reined in by the Executive Committee, he didn't "want to come off half-cocked," but he felt that MIT, in choosing what he jokingly called "good architecture," was renouncing its commitment to "the principle of scientific management."[7] Bosworth, he wrote dismissively to another friend, was nothing more than "a beauty doctor."[8] Nevertheless, Freeman, risking public embarrassment, finally let the matter rest, but about the old offer of the presidency of MIT, he confessed the following:

> I sometimes feel that I failed in my highest duty in not following the earnest suggestion of yourself and Pritchett a few years ago as to undertaking the management of this institution. I had, and still have, grave doubts about my possibilities in the dinner jacket end of such a job, but I believe that for one thing, the present waste would not have occurred, and I would, above all things, have delighted to try to introduce as many as possible of the principles of scientific management into the educational methods and machinery.[9]

Freeman did hope to use his research to write a book on campus design:

> Probably my dreams will not come true, but because of the great interest that I acquired in this matter of efficient college architecture and the many examples of the opposite kind which are coming into existence from year to year, I have been dreaming about selecting from the large amount of material that I collected numerous examples to illustrate my points and theories and writing a discourse of a few hundred pages under the general caption of "College Architecture."[10]

Freeman was urged to meet Bosworth, which he finally did in May, after first sending him a set of documents relating to "Study No. 7":

> I found him a very charming companion during our two hour talk, but plainly he and I have been educated in different schools. . . . I fear that the atmosphere that he has been breathing for twenty years is so super-celestial that nothing which savors of the factory and the intensely practical would satisfy him.[11]

Freeman never wrote the planned book, and his bitterness lingered for decades and was passed down in family lore. Even late in life at the end of his brilliant career, when he composed the four hundred pages of his autobiography, he pointedly made no mention of his MIT proposal.[12]

The Gentleman and the Architect

Unlike Cass Gilbert, Charles Follen McKim, and other leading architects of the time who diligently promoted their work and that of their firms, Bosworth never had the ambition for a nationally known office **[63]**. He saw himself as both a gentleman's architect *and* a gentleman. His polite and deferential demeanor as well as a highly developed sense of his own breeding were qualities particularly attractive to the likes of Rockefeller and Vail, who shunned the gaudy display and social pretensions of some members of their class. Bosworth's neoclassical aesthetic also appealed to them, as it spoke of control, restraint, and timeless validity.

A 1915 photograph is very revealing in this respect **[64]**. It shows Bosworth with Vail, J. P. Morgan Jr., and William Rockefeller, brother of John D. and president of the City Bank of New York, at the so-called Club Cottage on Jekyll Island, Georgia, a winter vacation spot for the rich.[1] William Rockefeller owned a private apartment next to the clubhouse, and it was there, in 1910, that they and others discussed the need for a Federal Reserve Bank in which a federal agency with oversight over the banking industry would be put in control of the nation's banks.

The occasion for the meeting depicted in the photograph here was a more public event: the first AT&T transcontinental telephone call between New York and San Francisco, via the Jekyll Island Club House, of course. Bosworth had been called to Jekyll Island to make some alterations to William Rockefeller's apartment.[2] The two events probably coincided. Next to Bosworth stands Samuel Breck Trowbridge (1862–1925), whose firm Trowbridge and Livingston had designed the Morgan Guaranty Trust Building, the headquarters of J. P. Morgan, in 1913.[3] Trowbridge, like Bosworth, had studied at the École des Beaux-Arts and was also a member of the Society of Beaux-Arts Architects. The photograph thus depicts Vail with his architect and J. P. Morgan with his at the moment in which their new buildings were conceived under the auspices of the muses of the classical past sanctioning the brave new world of telecommunication and finance of tomorrow. Today we might see a conflict between design and technology, and between a building that quoted the past but was to serve the future, but for the likes of Vail, Morgan, and Rockefeller, this was no paradox at all.

63

63 Bosworth with draftsmen in his New York studio,
ca. 1913. Bosworth is standing
in the front row, next to the
seated woman.

64

The photograph also gives us some insight into Bosworth, the man. Rockefeller, Vail, Morgan, and Trowbridge are all wearing crumpled and even ill-fitting suits while Bosworth is not only elegant in his highly starched shirt and immaculately ironed pants but also understands the logic of a black-and-white photograph. Ever aware of his environment, he even knows to look at the camera. A fastidious appearance was important to Bosworth not only as personal expression but in respect to architecture as well. Later, when designing MIT, he would argue that the planned statue of Minerva in front of the building was like "the neck-tie" that one should always wear when appearing in public. Formality for Bosworth had an important civic function, and the fact that the Minerva statue was never commissioned by MIT remained for him a lifelong disappointment.

64 William Welles Bosworth, Samuel Breck Trowbridge, Theodore Newton Vail, J. P. Morgan Jr., William Rockefeller, Jekyll Island, Georgia, 1915.

Bosworth's Designs for MIT

Bosworth, who had received the commission purely on the merit of recommendations, and who had actually never designed anything as complex as a university campus, had to work rapidly. He traveled to other campuses to study the problem, but unlike Freeman, who made a study of 2,000 buildings, Bosworth focused his attention on only a few, such as McKim, Mead, and White's Low Memorial Library at Columbia University, which had been completed in 1898.[1] He also studied the proposals of his forerunners, Child, Despradelle, and Freeman. He gleaned that MIT wanted a grand central building and a unified design plan, that there should be allowance for future growth, and that the campus should be divided into zones. Bosworth also saw the shortcomings of the preceding plans. Child's plan was clearly underdeveloped from a design point of view. Despradelle failed to adequately differentiate academic buildings from dorms, and Freeman's building, equipped with standard classical afterthoughts and add-ons, would have given the campus, despite all its functional innovations, only a perfunctory semblance to the great classical traditions of architecture. Bosworth's plan was a logical response to these insights.

By the summer of 1913, his initial scheme was ready and formally accepted by MIT on July 25 **[65]**. Comments and suggestions were made, a revision was presented in the fall, and on November 8, Maclaurin unveiled the plans to the public **[66, 67, 68]**.[2] Bosworth's building had, besides a magnificent grand court, a central, domed element and a multi-armed layout that could easily be expanded. Furthermore, whereas earlier projects had more or less assumed a common height to all buildings, Bosworth gradated the buildings toward the center. The buildings along the river had a two-story-high pilaster order, with the third story embedded in the frieze, but the buildings around the central court had a three-story pilaster order. This, of course, led up to the drama of the dome and the portico under it.

Another welcome aspect of Bosworth's design, not really addressed by any prior submission, was the successful integration of the dormitories into the main building complex. Freeman had relegated the dorms to Vassar Street, disconnecting them in form and geometry from the architecture of the main building. Despradelle in turn had integrated the dorms so tightly into the

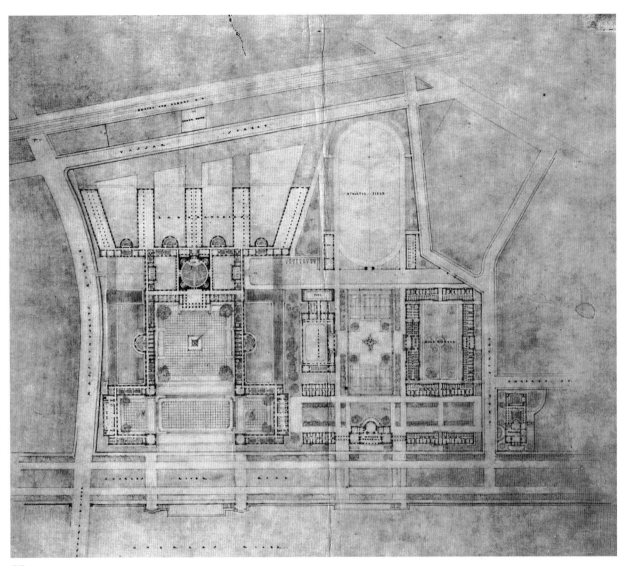

65

65 First plan for the projected MIT campus, William
Welles Bosworth, summer
1913.

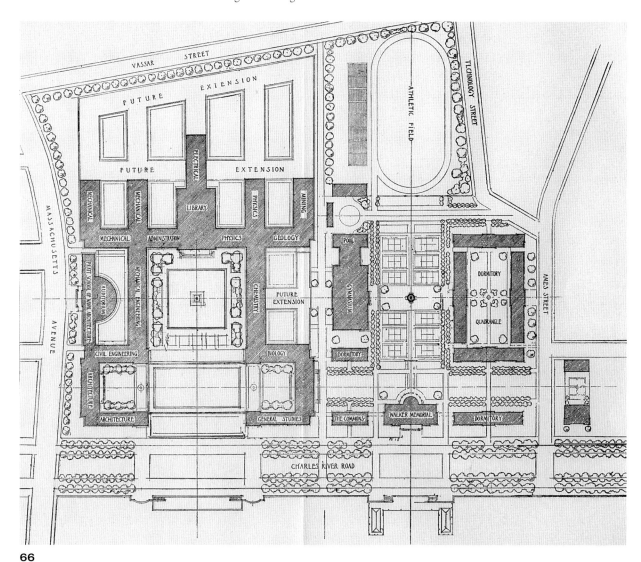

66

66 Plan of the proposed
buildings for MIT, fall 1913.

67

68

67 Presentation drawing of the proposed MIT academic building, William Welles Bosworth, fall 1913.
68 Watercolor presentation drawing of the proposed MIT campus, William Welles Bosworth, 1913.

scheme that they became practically invisible. Bosworth solved the problem by dividing the site right down the middle, with the academic buildings to the west and the dormitories and sports fields to the east, allowing plenty of room for their varying functional aspects. In his first scheme, he placed the dorms in a five-story-high rectangular *castello*. In the revised version, he softened the distinction to create a more unified plan. Particularly brilliant was the inversion of the orientation of the two areas. The institution, with its large courtyard, faced southward to Boston, whereas the dormitory part of the campus was to have an open space before it that stretched northward toward Cambridge. Accommodating first the tennis courts, it ended in the football field and was sealed against Charles River Road by the Walker Memorial building. The two parts of this whole were articulated at the river's edge by differently shaped landing docks. It was a simple and yet ingenious solution.

In a further show of mastery, Bosworth interconnected east and west by two sets of cross axes. The major axis began with a large auditorium to the west and moved through the Grand Court, with the statue of Minerva enthroned at the center, through the middle of the gymnasium and into the dormitory quadrangle. The second cross axis, a minor one closer to the Charles River, proceeded through the small courtyards of the academic building past Walker Memorial and ended in the cloistered garden of the President's House, the easternmost element of the whole composition.

The idea of two zones facing in opposite directions but stitched together by cross axes had been foreshadowed by Bosworth's solution for the Rockefeller estate, where house and forecourt face east and the garden next to the house faces west. Evidently, MIT's needs lay not only in excellent laboratories but in providing a rewarding human experience for faculty and students and a degree of representation deserving of the aspirations of a major American institution.

Bosworth-Freeman Synthesis

The difference between Bosworth's first and last plans is particularly illuminating as the changes reveal a gradual accommodation to many of Freeman's concepts, which were apparently worked into the plan over the summer of 1913. The first plan was more typical of Beaux-Arts design conventions. Corridors, for example, ran along the inside walls of the façade of the buildings as was standard practice during the nineteenth century, when lack of ventilation made corridors unpleasant. Practically no French Beaux-Arts building had corridors running through the center of the building. By the turn of the nineteenth century, however, with the emergence of ventilation systems and electric lights, the double-loaded corridor came into its own and was used with particular effectiveness in schools and government buildings. With his faith in modern technology, Freeman had, of course, never even considered anything else. In fact, the double-loaded corridor was the central element of his design.

Bosworth, too, was of course quite familiar with the double-loaded corridor since he had used it effectively in the Scarborough School. But unlike Scarborough's corridor, the MIT corridors were stacked on four floors and had no access to roof skylights and exterior ventilation. Bosworth, therefore, fell back on French models. Nevertheless, sometime between the first and second plan, Freeman's argument sunk in, so much so that, with the exception of the façade, the plan, with its wide corridors, high ceilings, concrete frame, lightweight interior walls, and generous staircase lightwells, began to take on the unmistakable imprint of Freeman's layout. In fact, photos taken during construction reveal the building's extraordinarily modern, open-grid, concrete structure with crossbeams supported by pairs of columns in the middle, just as Freeman had envisioned it [69, 70, 71, 72, 73].

One of the few places where one can today get a sense of the concrete system is in the staircase of Building 2. Its clean lines and luminous interior prefigure the Bauhaus ideals of the 1920s.

The successful importation of Freeman's ideas may have been facilitated by Freeman's friend Charles A. Stone, the engineer MIT had chosen to work with Bosworth. Stone, also an MIT graduate, was co-president of Stone and Webster Inc., one of the largest construction companies in the United States.[1] He was also a financial contributor to the MIT project to the tune of $500,000

69

70

and could tap into important social connections in the New York business community. In 1916, for example, along with Vail and Vanderlip, he served as a board member of the American International Corporation, which promoted American businesses abroad. Though he was a member of the Executive Committee, he was chosen to head the construction of the MIT buildings by a special committee consisting of Coleman du Pont, George Wigglesworth, and Vail.

Stone developed a most amicable relationship with Bosworth and not only asked him to design his house and gardens on Long Island, but also helped Bosworth to acquire a property next door to his own in that prestigious area. Freeman, however, presumed that Stone was in his camp, indicating to a friend in a letter that Stone "is working with all his might and resources to try to pull the situation out of the hole."[2] In the end, Freeman claimed, not with-

71

72

out some bitterness, that between "twenty-five to fifty percent" of the building was based on his suggestions.[3] Stone's contribution as a mediating agent, however, must also be acknowledged. He understood that the ideal relationship between architect and engineer necessitated a degree of cooperation and coordination to result in the perfect and frictionless symbiosis evidenced in the MIT building.

71 Building 8 under construction, 1915.
72 Building 10 under construction, 1915.

73

73 Room on first floor of
Building 2, 1916.

Between the Lines of Modernity

Of all the major campus commissions in the United States, and there were indeed a goodly number, MIT's was among a mere handful designed at that time in an austere, classical style. It was also perhaps the only one with a direct, if largely unacknowledged, input from a civil engineer. This "input" came about in an unusual way, as we have seen, for it was not provisioned. Furthermore, given Freeman's inability to let go, it was almost derailed altogether. We can easily discern how wide the gap between Freeman and Bosworth was by their different backgrounds and the itineraries of their careers. Freeman, raised on a farm in Maine, prided himself on his hardy New England stock. Caustic and unceremonial, he believed in reason, progress, and thrift. Bosworth came from a long American lineage going back, so he claimed, to a Frenchman who had arrived with the English settlers on the *Mayflower*.[1] Although Bosworth did not flaunt his social status, it was a point of legitimization nevertheless in the world of the Rockefellers and Vanderlips in which he moved. The difference between Freeman's and Bosworth's respective approaches was, however, not only one of social background but also one of the conflicting disciplinary ideals the two men represented.

Freeman's simplistic view of architecture as a field concerned only with appearances may have been something of a caricature, but the truth was that the practitioners of the Beaux-Arts style in the United States—by then securely entrenched in academe—were indeed slow to accept technological improvements. Although the architects of the time might have taken an interest in new building technologies, façades still had to express a reassuring continuity with the past. The architectural journals of the time clearly reflect this situation. The editors of the *American Architect*, particularly fond of Bosworth's architecture, for example, intermingle articles that feature Beaux-Arts designs with those of the latest advancements in concrete or steel construction with little discussion of how these two disciplinary environments might be coordinated. For this reason, their seamless integration in the MIT building, although largely unnoted, was remarkable.

In time it became evident that it was architecture that had to embrace the new realities, as materials, concrete, and, above all, steel were not only gaining respectability but were also demanding to be visually acknowledged. In the United States, however, it would not be until the late 1940s, under the influence of immigrating European architects, that steel and concrete were frankly acknowledged and allowed to surface as part of the architectural vocabulary. Why America came so late to this realization is a story for another book, but it was in Germany that the first cracks in the edifice of academic classicism appeared, perhaps partially because the full-fledged Beaux-Arts school system had never quite been so fully accepted there as in England and the United States. We should also consider the German architect and theorist Hermann Muthesius (1861–1927), who, in his 1913 article "The Problem of Form in Engineering," succinctly summarized the very same problems plaguing the design of the MIT buildings.[2] Muthesius, much like Freeman, acknowledged the difference between "use" and "beauty," but he argued that the former possesses its own type of aesthetic and that architects should learn to work with that aesthetic rather than relegate it to a lesser level of design. Obviously, the Taylorist school of thinking to which Freeman subscribed had not yet theorized itself in this way in the battle against established habits and expectations. It had, in other words, not yet understood the aesthetics of functionality. With the exception of Frank Lloyd Wright, it took many years before U.S. architects broke with tradition in matters of style.

It would, however, also be wrong to consider Freeman the harbinger of the up-and-coming and Bosworth the late representative of an architecture slated for extinction. Both were in their complementary ways part of the modernist story line. Rockefeller and Vail had redesigned the American banking system by creating the Federal Reserve Board, and Fish, one of the leading patent theorists of his day, had instituted the patent system under which AT&T was to flourish for decades. AT&T especially was in the forefront of that new business world that combined secretive behind-the-scenes practices with the need for highly visible corporate identities. Bosworth knew how to deliver the representative imagery that summarized and glorified corporate achievement. By contrast, Freeman's world was built around the practical principles of Taylorist transparency and hands-on control on the factory floor. His gamble did not pay off partially because MIT's mission as defined by Maclaurin was about more than just producing technological graduates. It is true that MIT hesitated while it tried to define its role for the future, but once its vision had been clarified, Maclaurin came down without further hesitation on the side that accepted the importance of representational imagery.

But there is no denying that many of Freeman's suggestions found their way into the project under the overall umbrella of Bosworth's aesthetics and that Bosworth with his ear to the ground accepted with dignity many of the novel engineering features such as the corridor, the concrete frame, the Taylorist ideology of efficiency, and the natural illumination designed from "inside-out." The result speaks for itself. More than many buildings from that era, it has aged remarkably well.

The Grand Opening

For over a year, MIT celebrated with drawings and photographs [74] its construction as it rose gleaming white on the shores of the Charles River. The triumphant celebrations that finally marked the opening of the New Tech lasted for three days, ending on June 12, 1916. A chartered steamer brought alumni and friends from New York City, an automobile caravan brought hundreds more from upstate New York, and untold numbers of would-be participants arrived by train. There were speeches, dances, beach parties, and nautical events. Among the guests of honor were Alexander Graham Bell, Orville Wright, Henry Cabot Lodge, and Franklin D. Roosevelt. George Eastman was

74

74 A drawing in the MIT yearbook of a view across Charles River of MIT.

75

there, and he raised his glass in a toast at a glittering dinner party to the elusive donor, "Mr. Smith." AT&T—the corporation behind the institution—made its presence felt by creating simultaneous transcontinental telephone exchanges of the thirty-five MIT alumni clubs around the country, the first telephone conference ever [75].

The highlight of the celebration was a dramatic night procession of students and faculty members that proceeded from the old MIT building on Boylston Street to the spacious Grand Court of the new building.[1] The festivities had been designed by one of Boston's best-known and certainly most colorful architects, Ralph Adams Cram, who just a few years earlier in 1914 had attained professorship at MIT. Cram threw himself into the celebration with gusto and marched in the procession as Merlin, the Magician [76].

The procession was led by Richard Maclaurin and James R. Munrow, the secretary of the Corporation, who was carrying a small box containing MIT's seal of incorporation. They were followed by a group of students carrying a large chest holding MIT's charter and archives [77]. Then came an escort of undergraduates dressed as Venetian guards, who in turn were followed by the

75 Telephone dinner of the Pittsburgh Alumni Association on the eve of the opening of the MIT campus, 1916.

76

76 Merlin, as played by
Ralph Adams Cram, 1916.
77 Scene from the opening
ceremony, 1916.

77

78

78 The *Bacanteaur,* designed by Ralph Adams Cram, 1916.

rank and file of students, all decked out in various costumes. Leaving the Rogers Building at dusk, the procession made its way in ritualistic silence to the shore of the Charles River, where it boarded a lavishly outfitted boat, also designed by Cram **[78]**. It was modeled on the famous *bacanteaurs*, the barges of the seventeenth and eighteenth centuries that carried the Doges of Venice across the canals. Its captain was Henry Morss, dressed as Columbus; he was an important figwre in the hierarchy of MIT, a celebrity yachtsman, and winner of the Bermuda race of 1907. The barge featured Mother Technology as figurehead, holding a torch in one hand and what appears to be a photographer's lamp in the other.

As the boat, dangerously overloaded with its cargo of professors and students, pulled away from the shore into the darkness of the night, noise bombs signaled the searchlights stationed on top of the new MIT buildings to train their beams across the dark waters of the Charles River to illuminate the *Bacanteaur* and guide it to the Cambridge shore. Having crossed the river, the group proceeded to the Grand Court to the music from Grieg's "Land Discovery." Once all the distinguished guests had settled into their canopied perches and Samuel W. McCall, the governor of Massachusetts, had arrived on horseback escorted by two troops of Lancers dressed in scarlet uniforms, the scene was set for one of the most spectacular public events Boston had ever seen: an outdoor performance of "The Masque of Power."

The "Masque," featuring the noted dancer Virginia Tanner and her troupe, involved more than a thousand student and faculty participants **[79]**. The musical accompaniment was delivered by a chorus of 500 singers and an orchestra of 100 musicians.[2] The costumes were specially designed for the event by Charles Howard Walker, a noted Boston architect and educator in the decorative arts. Steam machines were brought in to blast out mists that in turn were illuminated by colored lights from hidden high-power lamps, all engineered

79

 DEDICATION WEEK

a deafening noise of bursting bombs the faculty disembarked, carrying with them the Charter and Great Seal of Technology.

The landing was immediately followed by the performance of "The Masque of Power," the Pageant in eight episodes written for the occasion by Mr. Cram and played by more than seventeen hundred people, most of whom were students. The beauty and significance of this wonderful spectacle has hardly been equaled in history, and from the time when Chaos appeared in the court, to the singing of the "Star Spangled Banner" at the conclusion, the audience sat spellbound, wondering at the magnificence of it all.

The Pageant is best described in the following excerpt from the program.

The Masque of Power

First Episode

Chaos. In dim light and through dull vapors, somber shapes, shot with comet-like flashes, move dizzily to dissonant music. The mass billows and heaves until it discloses on its crest the Time Spirit; the turmoil quiets, the Elements separate, the music and lights soften to a brooding calm. Order comes out of chaos.

Second Episode

The Dance of the Elements. The light brightens, and on seven thrones around the arena are seen the Six Elements, with the Time Spirit in the midst; each Element surrounded by groups of satellites. The Dance of Earth is first, followed by Water, when slim fountains spring up around the dancers. Air, as the Storm, is next, with Electricity. Then comes the Dance of Fire, which at last is combined with Water, out of which blending comes the Dance of Steam. At the mandate of the Time Spirit the Elements and their satellites mingle in the Dance of Created Things.

MISS TANNER AS THE TIME SPIRIT AND MR. CRAM AS MERLIN

56

Third Episode

The dance dissolves, the Elements returning to their thrones. From the outer darkness creep huddled groups of Primitive Man; the dull figures crouch terror-struck and sing the Hymn of the First Fear, a groaning Litany. Out of this comes the first worship, which centers around Fire on his throne. From the midst of the barbarian mob springs Prometheus, who leaps on the throne of the god, seizes the torch from his hand, and brings it down to his fellows, who overwhelm Fire, cast him down, and seat Prometheus in his place. The

79 Virginia Tanner and Ralph Adams Cram, 1916.

80

by the same firm that had created the much-admired night lighting of the Pan-Pacific Exposition in San Francisco in 1915.

The first act opened to a shadowy scene, with rumbling music representing Chaos. This was followed by the Dance of the Elements—air, water, fire, and earth. Man arrives on the scene and vainly tries to master the elements until Will and Wisdom arrive to lead Man through the historical ages, with each age contributing its share of Progress. Out of a dark corner, however, there suddenly appear Greed, Selfishness, and War. Just as all seems lost, a light bursts through a rift in the clouds, and there stand the figures Righteousness, Will, and Wisdom. They defeat War and help Man overcome the Elements to reign supreme. Merlin then makes his entrance to the sounds of Triumph and leads the forces of civilization, century by century, to the throne of MIT's alma mater. The hymn to the New Technology was sung, and the flag was raised.

As a final good-bye to the old building, one of the searchlights raised its beam into the air until it crossed in the sky with the searchlight on top of Old Rogers. Then, slowly, the two lights died out, leaving everything in blackness except for a single shaft of light rising skyward from the new courtyard [80].

80 Illustration of the closing of "The Masque of Power" at the opening ceremony, 1916.

part two

Architectural Notes

The Campus Plan

Although campus architecture is a significant part of the history of American public architecture, there can be no doubt that the period from the 1880s until the First World War represented a high point. In fact, after skyscrapers, the campuses of that period, MIT's included, are the most lasting architectural achievements of the age. At MIT, the buildings' single mass, derived from German models, differentiates it from McKim, Mead, and White's 1894 master plan for Columbia University in New York [81], Gilbert's 1908 plan for the University of Minnesota in Minneapolis, and even Paul Cret's plan for the University of Texas of 1933. All were composed of rectangular buildings, as were most campuses of the time. Furthermore, at MIT, the decision was made to avoid designing the campus as a collegiate retreat as was then fashionable. Between 1878 and 1905 Harvard Yard on the north and east was surrounded by Charles McKim's Memorial Fence. At MIT, the large court, facing the river and the Boston skyline, emphasizes the institution's openness to the urban environment and fulfills Maclaurin's ambition that the Institute stand "as noble an ideal as any that can be expressed by form."[1]

It is not only the representative aspect of MIT's academic building that is so impressive. Few if any academic buildings of that era could, in their construction, be considered as advanced as MIT. Freeman's factory aesthetic would years later be celebrated as "modern" in the work of Walter Gropius and Le Corbusier. In the United States in 1916, such a modernity had not yet been identified and appeared in public buildings only in the form of largely invisible construction elements, but its presence at MIT should at least be recognized. Finally, it is important to appreciate that, unlike many scientific buildings of that era that eventually had to be altered, transformed, or demolished to accommodate changing needs, the MIT building has resolutely withstood the test of time.

Because the MIT building was ultimately much more expensive than anticipated—partially because of the outbreak of World War I just one year into construction—only a fragment of the dormitory section of Bosworth's plan was completed. The resultant incoherence of the eastern end of the campus meant that later additions to the academic building could encroach into

81

the area initially reserved for living and sports. Nevertheless, the original
buildings and their design principles were for the most part respected, the
most dissonant exception being Building 9 by the firm Skidmore, Owens, and
Merrill, which interrupts the generous flow of the corridor system. This is not
the place, however, to discuss the post-Bosworth history of the MIT campus.

81 Columbia University,
view of campus, looking
north from 114th Street, ca.
1914. Photo by W. H. Wallace.

The Dome

As to the various building elements, the most obvious is, of course, the dome, which went through several design phases. The first scheme was modeled on McKim, Mead, and White's library at Columbia University in New York, a building Bosworth praised as a masterpiece in a lecture he gave at Columbia in 1911 **[82]**. Bosworth's design, however, had eight columns compared to the ten from McKim, Mead, and White's library. Bosworth eventually adopted the motif of ten columns, but he spread them farther apart and made them pro-

82

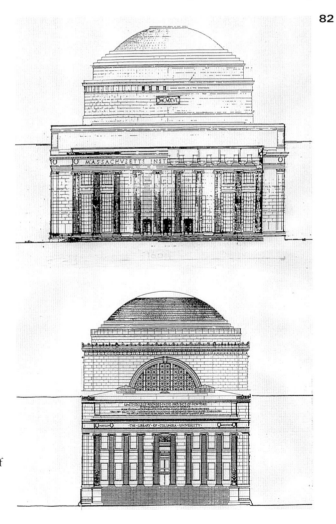

82 Comparison between Building 10 of MIT (above) and Low Memorial Library of Columbia University by McKim, Mead, and White (below).

83

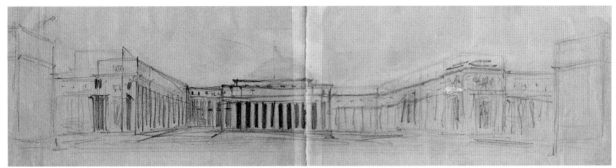

84

85

83 Paper, plaster, and clay study model of the proposed academic buildings of MIT, summer 1913.
84 Sketch study of central court of the proposed MIT campus, William Welles Bosworth, 1913.
85 Paper and plaster study model of the proposed academic buildings of MIT, summer 1913.

portionally taller to evoke a more stable and horizontal impression **[83]**. He also rejected the so-called thermal windows in the attic zone. Had the dome been built with the vast interior space initially planned, it would have been the largest indoor space in Boston. To study the visual effect of the dome from various angles, Bosworth used a clay model that allowed him to move the dome up **[84, 85]**.

In the first plan the dome was to contain a large assembly hall, but in the second, perhaps influenced by Vail's gift, it was reserved for a library **[86]**. Lack of finances eventually led to a reduced design, and for a while, it was even debated whether the dome should be built at all. To preserve it, a smaller, more

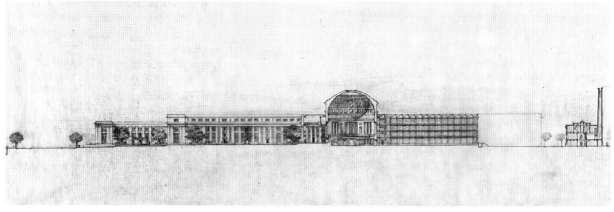

86

87

conventional, and awkwardly positioned lecture hall had to be designed for the second floor, while the library was located directly under the vault of the dome. Yet, the interior was not lacking in elegance. A capacious oculus admitted light into its center, and its perimeter was surrounded by a row of Corinthian columns. Four curved-topped aedicules added a counterpunctual element **[87]**.[1] More baroque in flavor than what one normally might have expected from Bosworth, the building seems in fact to be an inside-out quotation from Christopher Wren's St. Paul's Cathedral (1675–1711).[2]

86 Sectional study through the court and dome of "The New Technology," William Welles Bosworth, 1913.
87 Interior of Vail Library, undated.

The Portico

Only the most perceptive student of architecture will notice that the ten huge columns of the portico are not standing in a straight line **[88]**.[1] They form a slight outward curve so that the column at the center protrudes about nine inches more than those at the ends. Bosworth points out that he was inspired to this curvilinear baseline by William Henry Goodyear's book *Greek Refinements: Studies in Temperamental Architecture,* which was published in 1910. Bosworth had actually met Goodyear in Pisa and states in a letter that

88

88 Colonnade of Building 10.

Goodyear taught him "to avoid all perfect geometrical forms" and aim instead for "a softness of charm as mathematical exactness appears machine-like and without vibration."[2] Bosworth discovered that indeed the columns of the Pantheon in Rome are not set in a straight line either, but form a slight curvature. Current observation affirms this, even though the variance may be due to the columns' varying thicknesses. Bosworth also changed the distances between the columns, reducing them toward the sides. The central bay measures fifteen feet two inches, whereas the last one is fourteen feet three inches. Bosworth took great care to avoid that automated over-perfection that is often the death-knell of perfunctory classicism, something one might perhaps have expected from Freeman. He preferred to arrive at a sort of vibrating, living organism, an organic classicism, so to say.

In 1928, Bosworth designed a memorial for Maclaurin in the lobby. It consisted of a stele and benches placed close to the central door, but it was never executed.

The Court

The court, too, went through various phases, with the final design featuring a large, paved central courtyard with perimeter plantings. The space was composed of a rectangle that extended toward the river; it corresponded to the rules of the golden section. Between the two side courts was a rectangular piazzetta with two small fountains to create a series of thresholds, both real and implied, leading to the portico. The final design of March 1916 was turned over to designers in Olmsted's office for last-minute adjustments, and some tall cypress trees were added at the corners **[89, 90, 91, 92, 93, 94]**.

89 Bird's-eye drawing of the proposed MIT campus, William Welles Bosworth, 1913.

89

90

91

92

90 View into main court, 1913.
91 View of MIT building from central court, 1913.
92 Central court of the proposed MIT campus, William Welles Bosworth, 1913.

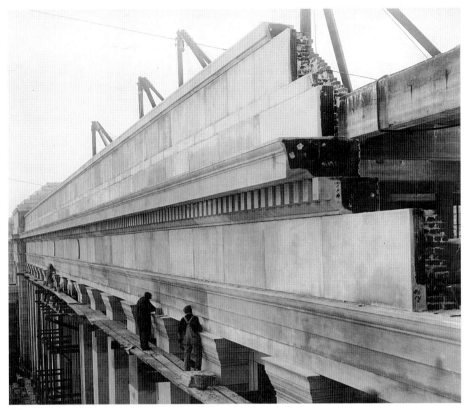

93

93 Cornice under construction, 1915.
94 Building 10 and court after completion, 1916.

94

By 1928, Bosworth's court was in serious need of repair. At the center of a redesigned court, Bosworth now envisioned a grand reflecting pool. The plan was rejected. Instead, the central part was ripped out and the entire area was planted with grass and trees so that the space eventually became something akin to a park, as it is today. The rhododendron bushes, which were part of the original planting scheme, were left along with the perimeter walkway. Regretfully, the bushes are now so overgrown that they threaten the delicate visual balance Bosworth had envisioned between foliage and architecture. In 1974 the court was named Killian Court after MIT president James Rhyne Killian Jr.

The Statue of Minerva

The initial plan had provided for a three-story-high statue of Minerva but by 1937, when Bosworth designed the Massachusetts Avenue entrance, funding had still not yet come forward. (See image 89.) This caused Bosworth considerable chagrin and he wrote repeatedly to his friend Frederick Gardiner Fassett (1901–1991), associate dean of students at MIT (1952–1966).[1] In one letter, written as late as 1961, the elderly Bosworth, in a shaky but determined hand, described the Minerva as the finishing touch, the "necktie" of the composition, pointing out that proper attire is mandatory for a building of such prominence. He argued that the statue as complement to Beauty was symbolic of the highest ideals. He wanted the commission to be given to his friend Paul Manship (1885–1966), with whom he had traveled to Greece and Egypt. In his eyes, Manship had proven himself at the AT&T building, and Bosworth's confidence in him was borne out when Manship did the famous Prometheus (1933) at the Rockefeller Center, a sculpture that clearly demonstrates the loss to MIT. Bosworth wrote pleadingly to Fassett and even noted that Manship had agreed to design the Minerva for a reasonable price. In 1922, Bosworth approached another well-known sculptor, Daniel Chester French, who, however, turned down the offer.[2]

Even though Bosworth might have succeeded in convincing Fassett, the president of MIT, Julius Adams Stratton (1901–1994), was opposed to the sculpture.[3] Stratton feigned ignorance about the sculpture on a visit to Paris but according to Bosworth must have known about it since "it has been shown in every drawing ever made of that Great Court."[4] Bosworth lamented, "I've always felt the importance of some decorative sculpture on any piece of art-architecture. Yet I've never so far succeeded in getting the MIT of Boston to spend a cent on sculpture."[5] Stratton was unmoved by Bosworth's pleas. In a 1961 letter to Bosworth, he wishes the aging architect well, but in an attached note on the copy that went to Fassett, he added that MIT would like to find some way to honor Bosworth, adding "anything except a statue to Minerva!"[6]

The Genesis of MIT's Ionic Capitals

It is important to dwell a bit on the design of the capitals of the columns, if only because in our modern age they are frequently discounted as mere accoutrements of "classical architecture." The monumental Ionic style grew in popularity in the nineteenth century and was used mostly on museums and civic buildings. In late-nineteenth-century Boston, the Ionic was certainly the favored style, and Bosworth no doubt wanted to continue the Ionian theme that had already been established by such public buildings as Boston's Symphony Hall (1900), Horticultural Hall (1900–1901), Harvard Medical School (1906), the Museum of Fine Arts building (1906), Langdell Hall of Harvard University (1906), the Opera House (1909), and the monumental colonnade of the Museum of Fine Arts building (1911). Bosworth apparently had the Greek temple of Athena Polias in Priene of 330 B.C. in mind. As in Priene, the cushion between the volutes slightly sags over the *echinus*. Furthermore, on the MIT building the eye of the volute is placed a trifle further out from the edge of the shaft, whereas in later Roman temples it was flush. Bosworth also modeled his columns on the proportion of the Priene columns. Both are, in width to height, 1 to 8.9.

MIT's columns have Attic bases, however, which consist of a torus surmounted by a scotia (concave molding) on which rests another torus. The model here was almost certainly another famous temple on the Acropolis, namely the Erechtheion (421–405 B.C.), dedicated to the goddess Athena, and thus in accordance with the Minerva statue planned for the court. Those bases, much like the ones at MIT, are noted for their unusually flat scotia and big *torus inferior* (the lower convex molding) **[95]**.[1]

The Erechtheion theme is also evident on the decoration of the cornice—one of the few decorative elements of the building, except that Bosworth moved the molding from the top of the frieze where it is on the Erechtheion to the *cyma* molding of the cornice **[96]**. Nevertheless, the characteristic alternating rhythm between palmette and acanthus blossoms is unmistakable, and the same theme appears in the decorations of the bronze door frames of the portico.[2] Bosworth changed the Erechtheion motif slightly by adding lion heads, apparently modeled from Priene. The columns, therefore, are Erechtheion-Priene hybrids. That they appear on a largely Roman-type building arises out of Bosworth's conviction that the Graeco-Roman style represented American architecture at its best.

95

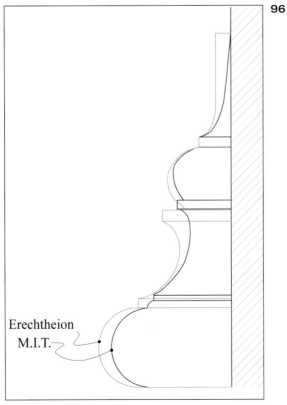

95 Comparison of MIT
Ionic order (left) and Priene
order (right).
96 Comparison of
Erechtheion and MIT Ionic
bases.

Walker Memorial, the Dormitories, and the President's House

As construction progressed, it became clear that the costs far exceeded the estimates. The $2.5 million became $7 million, a staggering increase patiently paid for by Eastman. Even so, plans still had to be scaled back. The dormitory quadrangle suffered the most from this belt-tightening, and its plans had to undergo significant simplification. The original plan had the Walker Memorial building at one end and the gym on the other. In between was a green with tennis courts flanked by dormitories. What was now at risk was the Walker building itself, at least as Bosworth initially had conceived it. Originally it had been planned in a relaxed classical style with a generous convex portico overlooking the Charles River. Its name was meant to honor General Francis Amos Walker (1840–1897), the third president of MIT (1881–1897), who had been an avid proponent of improved student facilities, the reason the Walker building was part of the plan from the very beginning. In preparation, MIT had created a commission in 1913 to study student life, headed by Henry Walter Tyler and Albert Farwell Bemis, both noted engineers, and the chemist Arthur Amos Noyes, acting president of MIT from 1907 to 1909. Their idea was to create a facility that would bind students closer to each other and especially to their alma mater. Although admittance was not to be based on social standing, it was to have the atmosphere of a gentlemen's club to reduce, so it was hoped, "the power of the small cliques," in order to make it possible for "a man of limited means" to participate in "the real privileges of institute life."[1]

The commission initially proposed that the Walker be placed along Massachusetts Avenue, but Bosworth, wisely, placed it in the more protected area along Memorial Drive. Bosworth did not adopt their notion of a compact axial arrangement between the Walker and the gym facing each other over a quadrangle. Instead the gym was pushed to the west to open up the north-facing axis that left open the space between the Walker and the sports field. But with the shortage of funds, and no doubt criticism from the members of the Walker Commission, this plan was simplified and modified to result in a more compact and traditional symmetrical arrangement as proposed by the 1913 commission **[97, 98, 99]**. The second north-south axis was thereby eliminated. But even this proposal was reduced for an even more compact arrangement in which Walker was turned ninety degrees so that its narrow side faced

97

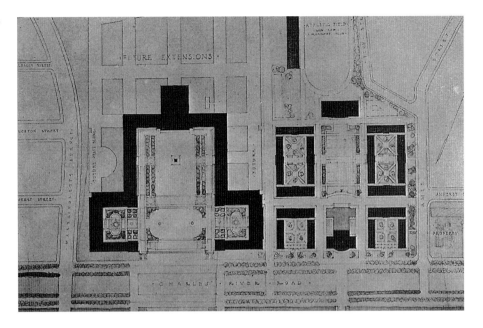

98

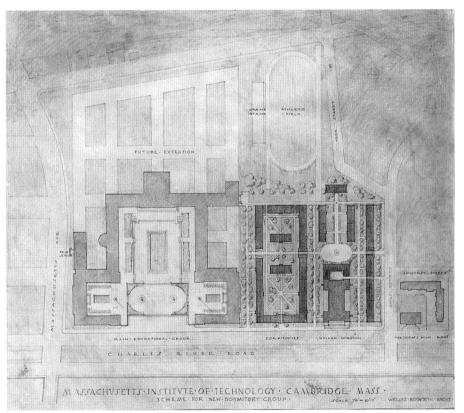

97 MIT campus plan showing revised scheme for the dormitory group, William Welles Bosworth, 1914.
98 MIT campus plan showing dormitory redesign, 1915.

99

Memorial Drive, with the result that the gym could be almost literally "clamped" into the larger framework of the dorm buildings.[2] When Walker was finished, MIT inexplicably reverted to the previous layout of the buildings, constructing first one and then the other dorm, now known as Senior House, resulting in an incoherence that later planners made no effort to repair.

By 1916 the Senior House was completed. It was an L-shaped structure in which Bosworth tried to preserve some aspects of the original *castello* idea. Its principal architectural feature was a Doric portico entrance with a loggia on the roof.[3]

The President's House, had it not come as a gift from Charles A. Stone, might never have been built [100, 101]. It was completed in 1917 and was the last part of Bosworth's plan to be constructed. It had a simple, rectangular plan with a garden at the back and a ballroom at the top. Framed on both sides by Senior House, it was shielded from the factories to the north.

99 View of proposed Walker Memorial building.

100

101

100 The dormitory and the President's House, ca. 1917.
101 The rear of the President's House, 1920s.

The Unbuilt MIT Chapel

Between Walker Memorial Hall and the President's House, Bosworth had originally planned a low gatehouse leading into the dormitory quadrangle. In the 1920s, he proposed a more ambitious project in the form of a chapel [102]. Disappointed that the monumental space under his dome had not come to fruition, Bosworth might have hoped to show off his skills with an interior space but this project, too, was not realized. The chapel, had it been built, would have been similar to the interior of the Columbia University library, except that it would have had two sets of paired columns and a huge bell tower lodged in one of the recessed corners.

102

102 Sketch view along Memorial Drive of a proposed MIT chapel, with the President's House in the foreground, early 1920s.

77 Massachusetts Avenue Entrance

In the late 1920s, when the MIT trustees began to think of expanding the institution along Massachusetts Avenue, Bosworth conjectured that the gap between Buildings 5 and 7 could be used for a court, set back from the bustle of Massachusetts Avenue. For the landscape design, he called in Jacques Greber (1882–1962), another Beaux-Arts graduate who had studied, like Bosworth, in the studio of Gaston Redon.[1] In the United States Greber had gained a reputation as a landscape designer, co-designing in 1917 the Fairmount Parkway in Philadelphia. Now, with Bosworth, he worked out a plan that would have opened automobile access for dignitaries by cutting a narrow roadway up to the entrance. This plan was also turned down.

MIT was, however, interested in Bosworth's alternative proposal, a grand entrance vestibule, for which a contract was signed in 1939. The vestibule was loosely modeled on the design of the chapel. It has a rather unusual plan consisting of two spatial structures: a portico and a lobby linked by a common set of columns. Toward the portico side, the columns are fluted, whereas on the inside, toward the lobby, they are smooth. Normally, neoclassical protocols would have demanded a reduction in scale from outside to inside, much as, for example, in the somewhat similarly shaped octagonal room in the Museum of Fine Arts. Designed by Guy Lowell in 1909, that room has pairs of Ionic columns that coordinate and emphasize the intersection of axes at the center of the building. The 77 Massachusetts Avenue building defies this Beaux-Arts tradition by fusing two monumentally scaled structures, with the result that the inner space remains at the less intimate urban scale. Perhaps Bosworth's experience in designing the Egyptian Museum in Cairo played a role in this plan. It had been commissioned in 1925 by John D. Rockefeller Jr. and was to be a gift to Egypt. Although never built, its entrance was a combination porch and dipteral vestibule. The vestibule of 77 Massachusetts Avenue, however, is domed and possesses champhered corners with pedestals that were to hold the sculptures of Aristotle, Archimedes, Ictinus, and Callicrates [103].[2] Predictably, the sculptural program was never filled, to Bosworth's undying frustration.

103

103 Sketch of interior of
Building 7, William Welles
Bosworth, 1928.

Appendixes

"Study No. 7" by John R. Freeman

In January 1913, Freeman presented his study to the Executive Committee of MIT. Included here is the talk he gave and his report, "Study No. 7." What survives of "Study No. 7," however, is not the report itself but his final set of notes, which are given in their entirety below. His drawings have been reproduced elsewhere in this book. Although some of the material between the lecture and the report overlap, there is enough difference that both are given here for comparison. Freeman's discussion about the boiler room and some suggested changes to Vassar Street have been excluded from this transcript.

Planning the New Technology:
"Study No. 7" by John R. Freeman, Engineer

Your chairman has told me that because of the important things that others have to say at this meeting, I can be allowed only ten minutes for telling my story and ten minutes more to show my plans, but [he] confesses that he has allowed an additional ten minutes as a factor of safety. It is hard to condense material that might furnish a whole lecture course into this brief period and I am compelled to begin abruptly and touch only the high spots as I proceed.

My part in this planning neither took the task at the beginning nor carries it to the end. Our faculty, experienced in the teacher's art and earnest that our college should carry its proud record into the future as without a superior on either continent, loyally began the work. A loyal group of young, enthusiastic alumni have helped to carry the study along. My part has been largely that of keeping others busy and helping to focus from divergent rays some things definite and tangible.

My "Study No. 7—subject to revision," which has been submitted to our Corporation and our Executive Committee and appears to have received their general approval, as somewhere near what we want, will soon be placed in the hands of one of the foremost American architects, one of our former students, whose well-proved gift of that special sense of proportion, line and mass which makes structures beautiful gives confidence that he will improve upon what I have done.

You must not take the drawings that I am to soon show you as the finality. They represent many months of earnest study and are almost complete enough so that contracts could be placed, but do not fail to understand that they show "Study No. 7—subject to revision."

For about twenty years I have been a trustee of Technology and on three different occasions have come nearer than my friends know, to entering academic life, and the present is not my first experience on a college "Building Committee." When traveling at home or abroad I have long found pleasure in inspecting technical schools and have enjoyed comparing with Technology the plants at Zurich, Charlottenberg, Munich, Crefeld, Milan and Birmingham, as well as many nearer home, therefore when ten months ago Mr. Charles A. Stone and President Maclaurin asked me to help in studying the problem of just what kind, shape and extent of buildings the Technology Corporation should construct on the new site, I welcomed the task.

My thirty-seven years since leaving Technology have been spent largely in contact with manufacturing plants and so first of all I studied this problem from the viewpoint of the industrial engineer, who plans his buildings *from the inside,* and first of all arranges things with a view to moving the raw material along the lines of least resistance and with the least possible lost motion, while it is gradually being shaped and smoothed up; always trying to obtain the utmost service from each thousand dollars invested in plant or talent.

In studying American college architecture, it has in many examples seemed to have been developed *from the outside,* on the theory that a college building was chiefly a monument which must look well from the street and that after first shaping up this outside satisfactorily the inside could be cut up into serviceable rooms without much trouble. About ten years ago, at the request of President Crafts, I made certain engineering studies of our Rogers and Walker buildings, which in regard to unit stresses, sanitation, fire hazard, and certain other matters, it has been just as well not to publish; and I will be equally discreet about what I have found in certain other colleges, of laboratory lighting deliberately sacrificed to harmony of exterior, of ventilation forgotten in a beautiful college building for chemical laboratories, of a great physical laboratory built in defiance of the requests of one of America's foremost physicists, that from the architect's standpoint it might be a more beautiful monument to the donor whose name it bears.

Much of my life work as inspector and president of certain fire-prevention insurance companies, has been occupied inspecting the seamy side of architecture, and it is but fair you should understand that I may have brought some unconscious prejudice to my present task, which kept me so long and persistently studying the inside rather than the outside.

The present problem is not altogether unlike that described to me by one and another of my friends, one a manufacturer of pipe fittings; the other, of tools, who in planning new factories, which they were determined should each be the best in the world for quality and economy of product, first had their several manufacturing foremen each devote weeks or months to sketching out the best possible arrangement for his own departmental machinery, regardless of relation to walls or support.

Next, the industrial engineer was given the problem of relation and of providing walls, windows, roof and foundation. So far all had been focused on efficiency; but next each called in an architect, men whose inborn sense of beauty in line and mass had been cultivated and ripened by years of experience, to the end that the aesthetic sense of all who passed or entered should be gratified.

THE FACULTY STUDY

Obviously, in our problem the counsel first to be sought was that of the members of our faculty. Each department head was asked by our President to confer with his fellow instructors in that department and each join in working out the best arrangement of which they could conceive, presenting this in a formal report, with detailed statements of floor space required for each subdivision together with plans, sections and elevations in outline for showing just what they believed was needed. They were asked to inspect other institutions and have frequent conferences within their department and to take two or three months' time so that the plans when presented should be fully matured. All reports were to be presented on sheets of standard size, to facilitate binding the several reports together in looseleaf files, so that the relation of one department to another could be most conveniently studied.

This work was entered into by the members of the faculty with great loyalty and enthusiasm, and in August last these reports had been brought together in three thick volumes, each of which was such an overflowing storehouse of facts, needs, comparisons and dreams of future greatness, that the first view was more terrifying than helpful to a trustee, particularly after one found that the separate requirements totaled to about a million square feet of floor space for 2,000 students; in other words, twenty-three acres of floors, all of which obviously should be as well lighted as a watch-maker's bench. On re-reading and reading again, these reports present each time some new light on the problem to be solved and the chief difficulty becomes one of finding how each can be trimmed down to a shape and size such that the aggregate will not cost more than the funds available and of finding out how all can be brought together on a fifty-acre lot and leave space in which Technology can expand during the century and more to come.

SOME NEW DEPARTURES

I have been much impressed that our lot of fifty acres is small for future needs and that its area must be most scrupulously economized. In my student days at "Tech," courses in Electrical Engineering, Electro-Chemistry, Public Health Biology, Naval Architecture, were not yet visible on the horizon. The growth of the next forty or one hundred years will surely call for similar new developments of art and science, and I have a vision of two particular lines on which a new departure might soon be made. The first was suggested to me four years ago when inspecting the technical school of Milan under the kindly guidance of Senator Columbo, the foremost engineer in Italy, who has given liberally of his time to the up-building of the school. He showed me the foundations of two new buildings, one which he had induced the paper makers of Italy to give, the other given by the soap makers, in partial carrying out his ideal that each great industry might have here a place to come for research in scientific principles of its art. At the famous engineering school at Karlsruhe, the German Gas Engineers have a similar relation.

What better way than this is open to make our institution still more useful to the industries of our country and what better way to increase the sympathy, appreciation and support from the great industrial community in which we live? When you examine Study No. 7, you will find sites suggestively reserved for certain great future buildings for post-graduate research.

The second suggestion is that of a larger summer school, partaking largely of the nature of a science college for teachers. Boston is an excellent summer resort and of such historic interest that everyone likes to visit it. Our unique and valuable plant has capabilities for further usefulness that should not lie in idleness four months out of the year. President Harper had similar views which bore fruit at the University of Chicago, and when studying conditions there not long ago I was told that in the summer classes were found the most earnest students of the year. How could the fame of Technology and the story of the opportunity offered by its laboratories and professors be more effectively carried to the bright ambitious boys in every corner of our land than by the teachers returning from such a summer school as might be held here.

Also the promotion of acquaintance and discussion among students and bringing more of brightness, cheerfulness, atmosphere and beauty into the school-day routine has been given much thought while drawing these preliminary plans.

Corridors of uncommon amplitude, well lighted, bordered by inviting fixed seat-benches on which small groups can meet for the five-minute interval between classes, everywhere abound. The general reading room is brought close to the center of things and given a broad inviting entrance, but most of all, as a meeting ground which shall long live in the graduates' memory as one of the bright spots on life's pathway, is provided a great cloister overlooking a broad garden filled with bright flowers fall and spring, with space for a thousand students grouped along the cloister seats.

"SCOUT SURVEYORS"

While the study by members of the faculty was going on, a second line of attack was brought to bear on our problem by the enlistment of from four to six alert young fellows, most of whom had recently graduated from Technology; for it seemed to me that some of the subjects operated upon by our lapidaries might have a different viewpoint from the professors and one which it was useful to develop.

The men selected for this inspection had mostly been seasoned by a year of practical work since graduation. They were armed with tape line, camera and memoranda of things to be thought about, and with letters of introduction to college presidents, and sent forth, East to Bowdoin, North to Montreal and Toronto, South to Virginia, Missouri and Texas, West to Illinois, Wisconsin, Minnesota, Kansas, Colorado and California; each instructed to see, measure and photograph and describe whatever he found that would be useful in planning the New Technology, and to give particular attention to all in the building line that was found useful in the social life of students.

Few appreciate the vast amount of college building that has been going on upon this continent during the past ten or twenty years. Great universities and scientific schools have been created *de novo* in many places; others like Technology, forced by growth to seek a broader campus, have built new and marvelous plants; others, particularly the great state universities, have expanded their scientific departments with a vigor and breadth of view and to an extent that few of us back here in the East have realized.

Never in the history of the world has so much building of colleges, technical schools and laboratories gone on as during the past ten or fifteen years, and some of our great industrial works and governmental departments have meanwhile established new laboratories, which must not be left out of the reckoning if one would be certain that this structure of tomorrow is to be fully the equal of what has been already built.

We recognized that some of the brightest minds in America had been working for ten years past on much the same problems that we at Technology now had in hand and were not surprised that our Scout Surveyors brought in a vast amount of useful material. I wish that I had time to show you the reports brought back from McGill, from the University of Toronto, from Texas, from Kansas, from Colorado, Minnesota, Wisconsin, Ohio, Pennsylvania, etc., etc. Everywhere we found much in plant and arrangement that was worthy of more careful study, and much recent college architecture that was very beautiful. Their reports comprise more than forty volumes of condensed information on costs per square foot and per cubic foot of typical buildings, of plans and photographs showing how the problem of the best shape of class room and lecture room, the most satisfactory floor covering, the best desk, the best laboratory tables, the best seating plan, etc., etc., had been worked out in different institutions. Everyone, President, Professor, Superintendent, Janitor or student, seemed glad to help Technology in this matter. We were given blueprints almost without number and in only a single instance did an architect hesitate when asked to give us blueprints of his working drawings. All of this material has been put into standard form for reference; all important blueprints photographed down to standard 8½ x 11 inch page, on which dimensions can be read with pocket magnifier and bound into the reports. The blueprints themselves have been arranged in filing cases, and the whole collection will be a most valuable addition to the Technology Architectural Library and will be useful from day to day, all of the time that the work of construction and furnishings is going on. Three copies of these reports were made, one for President Maclaurin, one to be passed around among the Executive Committee of the trustees, and one for my own further study.

DIGESTING THE DATA

This work of the Scout Surveyors also was mostly completed in September. Our next task was that of digesting and assimilating the mass of information presented in the reports of Faculty and Scout Surveyors, and the same men who had been serving as Scout Surveyors now took their places at drafting tables in my office, and together we worked over various possibilities of arrangement.

We resolutely set ourselves to studying the problem first of all from the inside and along the lines followed by the industrial engineer or factory builder, and having determined that the best of lighting and the best of ventilation were paramount considerations, and that in lecture rooms neither student nor professor should directly face the glare of the window light, we went to work to devise systems of unit construction, like those well-known in factory architecture, by means of which the cost per square foot of available floor space is brought down to the lowest terms.

It has long been plain to some of us whose calling takes us into the latest and best textile factories and machine shops, that under the strenuous competition and striving for excellence and economy, matters of window lighting, economy of service, ventilation, heating and transfer of stock in process from one operation to another, college architecture with here and there a notable exception, is twenty years behind industrial architecture in its efficiency, and so with plans of a hundred factories within convenient reach, we sketched, rubbed out, sketched again, tore up the sketches, started afresh, and again and again revised in the effort to devise these internal arrangements so as to give the maximum of economy, the best of light and the smallest amount of lost motion, before we began on the problem of the exterior.

I remember that a college vice president of great wisdom and success had urged the need of lecture room lighting such that the speaker could plainly see the expressions in the faces of his class and so discover if what he said was being taken in, and recalled that various professors had stoutly affirmed that it was bad ventilation and not what they were giving the men, which made most lecture classes sleepy or "dopey" at the end of half an hour being talked to. A few moments later, I will have some views put on the screen to show the means by which we hope to fix the responsibility for such results on something other than window light or bad air.

EXTERIOR

All along for ten months past, I had not wholly forgotten that our final design must be well clothed, nor that in order to be satisfactory, [it] must be beautiful.

Years ago, the chairman of the committee which built one of the most beautiful public buildings in America, told me that when the architect asked him his views as to style, he replied, "Give us a style that has proved satisfactory for about 2,000 years"; and remembering this, I wondered if in the marvelous developments of commercial buildings for office purposes in our great cities in recent years we could not find examples where the classic orders had been so modified so as to let in a flood of light, while preserving all that beauty of column, moulding and entablature which the Greeks of 2,000 years ago understood so wonderfully well. At odd moments and whenever opportunity offered, I cross-sectioned the office-building districts of New York, Boston, Philadelphia, Chicago, San Francisco, and some of our other cities, looking for types which could admit a flood of light and still be beautiful. Much was found to prove that this ideal of ample window light in combination with classic orders was possible.

Classic architecture at once suggests marble, granite or sandstone. Notwithstanding Mr. "Smith's" munificence, a million square feet of useful floor area housed in cut stone was plainly beyond our reach, nor did cut stone seem the most fitting material for a school where structural economy is to always be a fundamental lesson.

SYNTHETIC STONE

To a present-day Civil Engineer Portland cement concrete is the most natural building material in the world, and today it takes no very profound study to demonstrate that by this means we can bring the beauty of classic form within our financial limitations.

The Colonial house builder is not criticized for having brought these beautiful Greek forms of column and portico within reach by building them of wood, for thereby he added to the pleasure of life, and no one thought of a wood pediment or pillar as a sham or imitation. We will recognize in the building material for Technology not an imitation of stone, but greet it as the newest result of research in improved synthetic stone.

Portland cement concrete is preeminently the building material of the present epoch, and therefore is peculiarly appropriate for housing our great engineering school, providing only we can be sure of giving it a more beautiful exterior appearance than it commonly wears. The fact that nineteen out of twenty concrete buildings do not present a pleasing surface is, I am led to believe, after studying some hundreds of structures, not a necessary result of the use of this material. Altho [sic] Portland cement concrete has had nearly a century of practical use to test its resistance to frost and atmospheric corrosion, and for twenty years we have had under our feet in Portland cement sidewalks, examples of surfaces that do not crack or "craze" or suffer from the severe frosts of New England like the leaner mixtures used where massive strength is the only need, it very curiously is only within the past few years that the material has been faithfully studied and that our intimate knowledge of its properties has fairly begun.

The art of understanding of pouring concrete and of giving it a strong resistant and impervious surface has made wonderful progress within one, two and three years past, and there are abundant examples for proving that a rich, wet, fluid mixture can be given a smooth, impervious, durable and pleasing surface. The recent remarkable experiments by Mr. Logan W. Paige of the U.S. Bureau of Good Roads, upon concrete mixed with about five percent of oil, is suggestive of still greater progress in the near future in an impervious and frost-resistant mixture. Our Prof. Crosby, one of the most profound students of American building stones, tells me that concrete properly made should resist the gnawing tooth of time, frost and the coal-sulphur acids of city air, better than most marbles and sandstones.

Recent improved processes have greatly cheapened snow-white Portland cement and by the use of a crushed white granite or crushed white marble aggregate, given a very faint cream tint, smoke and time will bring an "old ivory" tint, and by means of special care in mixing and pouring and by joggling the iron molds while pouring is going on, we can now produce clean-cut shapes and smooth, impervious surfaces, that were hardly dreamed of five or ten years ago, and if after a century of exposure to frost and the acids and grime of city air, a fresh new surface is desired refinishing the exterior with a pneumatic bush hammer will always be a cheap and simple matter.

CONNECTED VERSUS DETACHED BUILDINGS

When one compares American technical schools with the great technical schools abroad, he is struck at once by the fundamental differences in the ground plan. On this side of the Atlantic, with two or three notable exceptions, we find detached and independent buildings, separated by broad areas of campus, across which the students must rush from one class room or laboratory to another, at frequent intervals thruout [sic] the day. In the principal European schools we find a single group of connected buildings commonly arranged around the four sides of a court yard or sometimes extended in an imposing façade, as at Charlottenberg. From these main blocks the growth of the past twenty years has in some cases compelled starting a new detached block, as for example in the recent Chemistry Building at Charlottenberg.

The reason for the difference in practice in America and in Europe is plain, but apparently it is not one which adds to the advantages of the

American school. This detached arrangement in America has come about in the older institutions by reason of their depending upon private munificence for support and by reason of their slow growth in their early days. It was not strange that when some friend of the institution found himself moved by generous impulse to donate a building, that the architect and the trustees should join in giving this building such a set-apart monumental character as would best perpetuate the name and fame of the donor.

In the great state universities, new buildings have commonly come one at a time and each for some special purpose, after a careful campaign for moving the members of the legislature to understand that a building for this particular purpose was the great special need of the time for making their college the most famous of its kind.

It is also not beyond the possibilities of human nature for the head of a department to take particular satisfaction in having a building separate from the others, devoted to his own field of study, which he naturally and properly regards as of preeminent importance and in which building he can, in a measure, be king.

I believe this detachment of buildings has worked strongly to the disadvantage of our American schools and I have been confirmed in this belief as I have day by day for many years watched students going improperly protected from the inclemency of the weather, from one building to another between classes. It is plain beyond all question that this detachment greatly adds to the cost of housing a given number of square feet of floor area and that it violates pretty nearly all economic rules.

In place of these I have sought to group the present undergraduate buildings in a great central mass and have found it possible to do this without sacrifice of light and with great gain in economy, efficiency and possibilities for ventilation and cooperation between departments and as I believe, with great advantage to the students.

In the central building a locker room with 1500 uncommonly capacious lockers is provided, in which each student who comes from outside the campus can leave his hat, overcoat, gripsack or other impedimenta, and as in commercial life be free from these impedimenta for the half day session. For the five or seven minute interval between classes I have as already stated, provided uncommonly ample corridors with permanent inviting seats, and have provided a beautiful cloister overlooking a spacious garden and with a doorway leading thereto from the general reading room, which is made as central and inviting as possible.

POWER PLANT

In many college group plans and in the early architectural studies presented to President Maclaurin, Boiler Plant and Power House was placed as far back in the rear as possible; as an unsightly and dirty thing. Surely a technical school should rather glorify and beautify and make its power plant one of its central and most attractive features, for it is the manufacture of power which most of all distinguishes the present epoch of human achievement, from all the ages which have gone before.

The power house, even the boiler house, can be made clean and beautiful by means of modern appliances, and I have given it a central and conspicuous position in the direct pathway of the student, and treated it as befits the most important of our laboratories.

My allotted time is passing and I hasten to show you some of the plans we have been making and a few illustrations to show the character of the data from other schools that we had to aid in our studies.

Notes on "Study No. 7" for New Technology (and various Studies made during the year 1912) by John R. Freeman, C.E. (Tech '76)

SOME GENERAL AND PRELIMINARY CONSIDERATIONS

This series of studies followed a series of studies by the Institute Professors for the housing and fitting up of the individual departments and an independent review of what was being done at other colleges.

For this later purpose a careful examination of the buildings and equipment was made at some forty prominent educational institutions comprising almost every college and technical school of the higher grade in the United States and Canada, chiefly by the corps of recent engineering and architectural graduates of the Institute, most of whom had received a preliminary training in the insurance surveys of the Factory Mutual Fire Insurance Companies.

These "Scout Surveyors" worked largely with camera and tape line, photographing and measuring the particular buildings at each college that appeared most instructive for planning "The New Technology." They conferred with instructors, mechanical superintendents and architects of these buildings, secured information regarding cost, reduced the building costs for purposes of comparison to the units of cubic foot of content and square foot of available floor area, and so far as possible secured blueprints from the working drawings from which the more recent buildings were constructed. (These hundreds of working blueprints will make a valuable addition to the Institute's architectural library.)

This information from faculty and surveyors was then assembled, classified and reviewed by the writer, who also personally inspected a number of the most noteworthy college buildings. The writer had particularly enjoyed a peculiarly intimate acquaintance with industrial architecture during the past thirty or forty years, in the course of professional duties as Consulting Engineer on buildings and repairs for various important industrial structures; and particularly close contact with industrial architecture in connection with the former duties as chief of the Inspection Department of the Factory Mutual Fire Insurance Companies, and had had occasion to critically study and compare the evolution of the latest types for textile factories, machine shops and paper mills in this country and England, as well as opportunity to study the seamy side of architecture. Immediately after the Iroquois Theater fire, he had devoted much time to study the construction of large auditoriums and particularly theaters. With a view to safeguarding life from the fire hazard.

FACULTY PLAN

Reference has been made to the studies made by members of the Faculty in planning the various departments. These reports and plans, with full details and explanations, as submitted to the President on sheets of standard 8½ x 11 size, make up three bulky volumes. The outline and the summary of their recommendations as to the floor space required are condensed on Sheet No. 51.

This group plan was made up by cutting out to scale, pieces of cardboard of the dimensions called for in the Faculty reports, for the several departments and planning all these pieces in the most compact logical relation to one another, so as to economize the area of the load to the greatest practicable extent and reserve space for dormitories and future buildings.

It is of interest to compare the area of the present Institute building with that of the proposed buildings, and to note from the table that in planning for an increase of about 20% over the present number of students in all departments, an increase of 200% in the floor area is called for.

EFFICIENCY AND ECONOMY OF MODERN FACTORY TYPES

Increasing keenness of competition in all that pertains to lessening the cost of production and improving the quality of product has led to a keener study of detail in window lighting, ventilation, and elimination of lost motion in factory design in the three classes named above, than in any other type of architecture. In many cases, conditions of mechanical efficiency, safety against fire and particularly window lighting, have been regarded as paramount and such scant attention has been given to exteriors that college architecture would hardly look to factories for their inspiration. The point of view of the industrial engineer and the mill architect has been so focused on the interior, and on the perfection of the single detail which should be repeated a hundred or a thousand times in the building group, thus reducing the construction costs to the lowest possible terms, that it has been fundamentally different from the point of view of the architect designing monumental buildings, particularly colleges, where too often beauty of outward form has been the paramount consideration and the interior and efficiency have been largely left to take care of themselves.

DIFFERENCE BETWEEN AMERICAN
AND EUROPEAN GROUP PLANS

The grouping of buildings and departments on the campus of the typical American college is remarkably different from that found in the most prominent European institutions. Here we find buildings of widely different architectural types scattered over a campus, each department, so far as possible, isolated and housed in a separate building so that the professor in charge of the department reigns undisturbed, largely in a little kingdom of his own, and the undergraduate student, in particular, spends some valuable time and runs much risk of colds in our northern climate, in passing from one lecture to another, and in many cases must hurry so to cover the distance and climb stairs within the allotted five minutes or seven minutes, that all opportunity for personal contact with the lecturer or for asking some questions, is lost. True, he gets the benefit of filling his lungs with fresh air, which becomes of great importance by reason of the wretched ventilation that commonly prevails in college lecture rooms and laboratories, but the process or lack of arrangement involves a waste that could hardly be tolerated in commercial life.

On the contrary, in the most noteworthy European schools, for example in the great engineering school in the suburbs of Berlin or the great Polytechnikum at Munich or the new group of buildings for the study of applied science at the University of Birmingham, England, one finds the departments so far as possible housed in a single, connected group, closely resembling the arrangement of the best modern factories. This plan has been followed on this side of the ocean in a few instances, notably in the recent buildings of the College of the City of New York.

The reason for this fundamental difference in ground plan is easily found in the fact that our American colleges have been mostly built up one building at a time, this one building being often provided for by some rich friend, in a way that naturally led the Trustees and architects to express their gratitude by making the building first of all a fitting monument to perpetuate the memory of the donor. It would be ungracious to criticize by name some of the college buildings in which I have been most hospitably received and where the troubled instructor has confidentially shown me how poorly suited the building was to the work done inside it and how, in disregard of his protests, it had been designed primarily to look well from the outside, and chiefly in order to give it what was imagined to be a proper dignity and harmony with its surrounding. This trouble is not confined to one part of the country, for I recall three very striking examples of this,—one near the Atlantic seaboard, another in the middle West, and the third on the Pacific Coast.

In one of these, the building honors the name it bears by being, as seen from the campus, one of the most beautiful monumental college buildings in America, but its interior is almost the despair of the men who have to work in it. Altho [sic] the professor in charge of this department at the time of the building of its new home was a man of exceptional ability, his expressed desires for abundant window light and convenient arrangement were not heeded. The monumental motive was paramount.

In another example, the professor-in-charge, when he protested that better light was needed than was promised by the plans in rooms where much work of dissection and microscopy was carried on, was told in effect by the architect that,—"What you ask for would upset the whole architectural unity of this campus. Can't you see that it is impossible to have anything other than Tudor-Gothic windows of moderate size in this place?"

In the third example, the devotion of the architect to a particular type of exterior and window setting within arcades has so darkened various lecture rooms that the lecturer cannot see into the faces of his class, an effect which is increased by placing the windows so that he must face them while lecturing; and in another room some of the windows are so set that a reflection from them occurs upon the blackboard behind the rostrum so as to preclude a large part of the audience from seeing what he has written thereon.

As a fourth example, I might cite a very recent large college building, devoted to the teaching of Chemistry, where all provision for ventilation was omitted until after the structure was otherwise complete, and where apparently the one leading motive was a beautiful exterior which should harmonize with adjacent buildings. The advice and protests of the professor in charge of the department, made before the work was far advanced, as he tells me, received scant notice. Of course a most eminent professor of physics, biology or chemistry may sometimes not be an expert in how to achieve structurally, the effect which he plainly perceives is necessary and only those experienced in the building arts can tell from a drawing just what the final structure will be like, and even with much experience surprises sometimes come.

I will not multiply examples, they are painfully plenty, both in America and abroad. They can be found indeed in the present buildings of our Institute, notably in the Rogers and the Walker Buildings.

About ten years ago, President Crafts asked me to critically examine these buildings. I spent afternoons for some weeks on the problem and I soon found unit stresses, fire hazards and lack of sanitary precautions sadly at variance with what it is presumed is taught to the students in those buildings. Thanks to Professor Lanza's alertness, numerous truss rods, not contemplated originally, were added to the Walker Building before occupancy, and the fire hazard in the Rogers Building to life and property was remedied so far as practicable, altho [sic] the conditions of the fire hazard today are such that insurance companies experienced in the study of fire hazards, well understand that nine-tenths of the better grade of cotton factories are far safer against having their use and occupancy interrupted for six months, than our present college buildings.

The writer has long had a curious fancy for inspecting college buildings and educational appliances at home and abroad, and has seen the inside of many of the most notable colleges in the United States, East and West, in Canada, Mexico, England and Germany; and after having studied the problem now in hand as above described, he became impressed with the belief that there was opportunity for a vast improvement in the efficiency of college architecture, and that after all, in items of first importance to the work to be performed, and using the term Architecture in its narrow, popular, modern sense, tho [sic] not in its true sense, the problem was about one-fifth architecture and *four-fifths a problem of industrial engineering.*

The best factories, with their painstaking attention to details for increasing efficiency and cutting down cost, are rarely built by architects in ordinary practice but are the work of specialists, like Main; Lockwood, Greene & Co.;

Makepeace; Brill; Coffin; Hardy; Ferguson; Steele; Dean and a few others, classified commonly as Industrial Engineers.

FIRST AN EFFICIENT INTERIOR;
THEN A BEAUTIFUL EXTERIOR

The writer, therefore, undertook these studies largely from the standpoint of the industrial engineer, to whom efficiency is a paramount consideration (but to whom beauty of form in every part should also appeal as worthy of most scrupulous attention, the subordinate of efficiency) and in the belief that *the problem must be worked out from the inside.*

First of all, we must obtain *a flood of window light;*

Second, *a flood of fresh air* under perfect control;

Third, an efficiency and *avoidance of lost motion* by student and teacher, equal to that which obtains in our best industrial works

And fourth, the consideration of the *psychology of student life,* the cultivation of the social instincts, the development of personal contact, must strongly control the layout of the very masonry. (Some fruits of this consideration will be found in the serious attention given to cloisters, cloister garden and to unusually ample corridors and entrance halls.)

Bosworth's Lecture:
"Mens Sana in Corpore Sano"

Bosworth gave his lecture "Mens Sana in Corpore Sano" ("A sound mind in a sound body") at Columbia University in 1911.[1] While Bosworth admitted in the lecture that society allows for multiple readings of this equation—"The scope of architecture makes room for all sorts of men because of the many classes of structures that our modern life requires"—he preferred an architecture, and, of course, an architect, that is good, healthy, and vital. The examples he gives are, among others, Trinity Church, designed by H. H. Richardson, and the library of Columbia University, by McKim, Mead, and White.

Bosworth's argument shows the emerging impact of psychology on aesthetic thinking. But psychology, for Bosworth, was not the search for personal expression as much as the understanding of the determinants that define creativity. Bosworth mentions, in this respect, graphology, the skill to interpret character based on handwriting, a then relatively new theory. A piece of architecture, he argued, will similarly reveal the architect "morally, mentally, and emotionally." In communicating with others, Bosworth writes, one should adhere to laws of proportion and order, since they are to architecture what good grammar is to speech.

The arguments Bosworth makes can be summarized as follows:

1. There is a direct relationship between one's personality and one's architecture.
2. Good architecture is dependent on good character.
3. What survives for posterity is the work of men with strong and vigorous personalities.
4. Architecture is not purely an art of personal expression but rather the result of the adherence to the laws of composition and proportion.
5. There are three grades of building that the architect is expected to produce: utility buildings, which require no level of art; houses, which require a discrete level of ornamentation and refinement; and the competition project, where art and utility go hand in hand. It is in the context of the latter that architecture makes its true contribution to society.

"Mens Sana in Corpore Sano"
by William Welles Bosworth

"Être architecte c'est être artiste, 'gentleman,' logicien."
VICTOR LALOUX[2]

When I agreed to come up here to give you a little talk, I made up my mind to say to you some of the things which I wish had been told to me, when I was where you are now.

It seems only a few years ago when I was myself sitting in a lecture room at the Institute of Technology, listening in a sort of bewildered wonderment to the men who talked to us, just as I may seem to be talking to you now. They told us about the unknown world of experience that somehow or other (I could not even guess through what channels) would develop out of those school days, into the professional life of a "real architect with a job."

I know so emphatically well!—what I wish those men had told me—and what I wish I had been influenced to do, that I mean to say it to you here today.

I remember how we used to spend our time mixing up the overshoes on a wet day, and playing nine-pins with the plaster statuettes and a plaster sphere, with a flat side, which was intended for a "shades and shadows" model; and we had only the faintest realization of what it meant to discourage Prof. Eugene L'Etang, who came regularly twice a week to criticize our designs, and found as a rule nothing to look at until the week before the "rendu." I never could feel wholly sympathetic towards him because he didn't adore the architecture of Trinity Church, then recently finished and the talk of the country.

But Prof. L'Etang never explained why he didn't admire it and we were even allowed to render some "projets" composed of stunted columns, and grotesque Romanesque architecture and colored to represent brown stone and granite.

All of us were discouraged from any thought of studying in Paris, and it was seven years after leaving the Institute, when I came to live in New York, before I realized that the methods of the École des Beaux-Arts (practically those which you are following here to-day) were necessary to fit one for those great opportunities towards which we all look forward. Only one other man of that whole number (who were at the Institute in my time) went to study in Paris; and he didn't enter the school.

Yet we deserved better! I know that you are given the best advice and the richest of advantages here; and it is all the more agreeable to tell you what I have learned to believe of prime importance, remembering that, though you may have had it said to you before many times, yet each one says it differently and each time you hear it you receive a different impression with a new impetus.

To begin with then I wish I had been told what I now regard as of first importance, that one's creation is an exact expression of himself!

That sounds very simple and perhaps is not new to you; but do you realize what it means? Someone has said "A man can't paint a picture bigger than he is." That doctrine I regard as fundamental. Every experience I have had has verified it. I see it everywhere. It involves the whole lesson of life and work, of development, of growth, of the relations between the body and the mind.

A man can't make a design better than he is! There's the pinch, in the fact that to him who knows how to read it, your work will always look just like you! If you express weakness, so will your work. If you express sincerity, so will your work. If you express nervousness and jerkiness, your design will show interferences of motifs. You will choose broken pediments and interrupted outlines as a natural result of your nervousness, whereas if you are robust and calm you will as naturally select stronger forms and masses, simpler surfaces, fewer motives and get carrying power in your principal shadows. If you are expressing weakness and evasiveness physically and morally, your designs will betray it in conflicting motifs and apologetic or imitative subterfuges; whereas, if you are a lover of frankness and honesty, your designs will be simple and direct expressions of the needs of the problem.

Someone has said: Tell me what you eat and I will tell you what you are. I say: show me what you are and I'll tell you what kind of architecture you will do. It is commonly admitted that handwriting reveals character. Design is the same principle in a larger way! Works of painting and sculpture more directly portray the physical aspect of their authors, because their forms are freer and more personal; but the architect cannot escape it, any more than the camel can escape his shadow. It will reveal him, morally, mentally and emotionally, just as his face does. We all learn in life to read faces. If you would change your facial expression, you know that you must change your mode of life, change your thoughts. So, I would say, first of all and with deep conviction: If you wish to do good architecture, develop good character! and don't stop there, but develop a healthy vigorous body.

That is as important as the good character for vital energy in any work of art, no matter in what form, whether it's a Rembrandt etching done with a needle—or a Michelangelo statue done with a sledge hammer—is the very essential quality that it must have to endure, to be permanently valued by humanity.

This theory has been verified to my mind wherever I have found works of art for many years. Men may value temporarily some delicate, die-away, poetical production of a morbid and neurasthenic brain; but never permanently! It is the vigorous works of vigorous men, such as the Victor Hugos, the Michelangelos, the Velasquez and Rubens and Cellinis, that survive longest and are most valued by posterity; the works of men of large personality and vital intensity.

Consider the work of the architects of today whom you know, and see how their work resembles their physical appearance. Even in the matter of refinement and cultivation it betrays them.

Could there be a better demonstration of the theory of resemblance between a man and his work than this one of Trinity Church in Boston and its architect, the late Mr. H. H. Richardson, in whose office I received my first impressions, and where I perhaps first absorbed the theory.

Note the strength of personality, of individuality in each; then the peculiar harmony between the nature of the man and the type of architecture he was attracted to, as well as the way he handled it. What failures his imitators made of it and how easy it is to see the reason why. Next compare the work which it is understood Mr. McKim did most personally—the Morgan Library—with the portrait photograph. Do you not discern as close a relation there between the two as you did in the case of Mr. Richardson and Trinity Church? First the general type of man and of style of architecture; then as compared with other buildings of its style, note the slight hesitancy of silhouette over the central motive, and see how the facial expression betrays a searching for the best. Small men usually write large and stand up straight, while tall men write small and stoop. But in design, a tall, thin man makes slim openings and high spacings, while the short, thick-set man likes broad low effects. These matters are entertaining and significant, but to resume the general question: What must one be then to produce a masterpiece? What are the qualities of a masterpiece? The answer to the first question is in the latter. One must possess those qualities. I should say first and foremost, strength (or vitality), life and energy, "vigorous handling'" as a foundation, is the absolute essential of a masterpiece! You will not find one without it; and no man can express it who does not express it in his personality.

The quality of next importance is judgment—common sense, defined by Dean Swift as "that perfect balance of all the faculties." Taine says that in a masterpiece one finds an expression of the idea, which is entirely adequate to the idea. Architecturally, this means that when one thinks of a private library for a "riche amateur," one cannot conceive of a more appropriate expression of the idea than Mr. McKim's Morgan Library; and so one accepts it at once as a masterpiece.

It means that when one thinks of Moses, one thinks of Michelangelo's statue of Moses—an expression "adequate to the idea." But in architecture in order that a building may adequately express an ideal, it is essential that the designer should not only be energized by vital power and controlled by sound judgment, but the application of a knowledge of the laws of his art is required of him as well! He must know how to make each part perfect, in order that the whole may be perfect—each link strong in order that the chain may be strong—just as an orator will be unable to control the thought of an educated audience if he makes mistakes in grammar.

The laws of Composition, regulating the relation of parts; the laws of Proportion, giving proper value to the separate features; the chief law of all, that the different parts and features shall form a Unified and Harmonious Whole: these are the indispensable qualifications in order that a work of architecture shall rise to the level of a masterpiece.

It is true that in art "not failure but low aim is crime," and that in order to do well one must always do his best; in other words, one should aim at Perfection: the Masterpiece.

In this connection, I am reminded of a remark made to me once by a Paris cab driver. I had taken him at the Louvre from which he probably inferred my interest in such matters, for on approaching the Opera House he turned round and waved his whip at the façade, saying, "Il faut l'esprit juste, pour avoir reglé tout ça; n'est-ce pas?,"—which might be translated as meaning, "He must have had a well-balanced mind to have controlled the designing of all that, eh?" Think of a coachman showing such appreciation.

And so, having analyzed the Masterpiece that I know each of you would like to produce in every design he creates, and having pointed out to you what my observations have persuaded me are required of the individual who succeeds in reaching that attainment, we come to the program of life as a whole for it is just like the program issued for a "projet."

There are two distinct "partis" to take: the one leads to Success as measured by the amount of work and the amount of profit; the other leads to the Success which is measured by the quality and tone of one's work.

Mediocrity is always in the majority. Mediocre taste, mediocre judgment, mediocre culture, mediocre health are the rule. It always has been so, except perhaps at the great epochs of art, and probably always will be so, while Distinction, by its very name, implies a quality apart from the usual, the popular.

At a Jury last week, some humorous member started a pool, the idea being that he who had voted for the largest number of the winning designs should get the purse. One of the members, on finding that he had lost, was overheard to say, "I should have been surprised and distressed if my opinion had been no better than that of the majority."

But remember that in the long run the world eventually takes the opinion of the best judges. For example, take the case of Rodin, the sculptor, whose work was over and over again rejected and ridiculed, but who now receives every honor that a sculptor desires. Amongst painters, think of Millet, whose works sold for a song during his lifetime and now bring fortunes.

In literature, most of the great plays and novels have been repeatedly rejected by managers and publishers, while temporary approbation is given to hundreds whose work is soon forgotten.

There are so many different branches of knowledge involved in the practice of architecture that one may get along fairly well if he is only proficient in some of them. The scope of architecture makes room for all sorts of men, because of the many classes of structures that our modern life requires. A curve might be plotted to show how the range varies from buildings where art alone dominates, as in commemorative monuments, to those where the appropriation covers only the cost of what use alone requires, allowing no balance for expressing euphoniously the uses to which the structure is dedicated; and, sad to say, there is still a lower grade of building which the architect is continually asked to produce, where the appropriation is actually inadequate to cover the reasonable requirements of use itself, and light and space and strength and durability and even safety are sacrificed on the altar of commercialism.

An English visitor put it that many of our buildings "couldn't be what they were even if they were what they appeared to be." He had seen some shop fronts in the Bronx with galvanized iron imitations of rock-faced brick.

But the problems by far in the majority are those where utility dominates and the client has little if any interest in beauty.

The relation between the cost and the earning power of his building alone interests him, as it is his sole motive for building. He starts and ends with the figures on the calculation sheet.

To succeed with that class of men (and a very worthy class it is in any community), the architect need have little if any education in the theory of architecture. Some experience in draughting and a knowledge of building methods, city laws, etc., will suffice, if he is a good calculator and administrator, and watches the "fashion" in building enough to imitate the latest type.

The next grade of buildings may be perhaps houses where utility should reign supreme but where art sometimes creeps in, but not if too much sought after. When pursued, you have here counterfeit, "ornamentation," instead. Contrast the most conspicuous house on Fifth Avenue with that ideal city house on the corner of Fifth Avenue and 49th Street, so admirably expressive of its uses, its comforts, its refinements; and yet so retiring with all its prominence as not to excite the notice of the most anarchistic of the passers-by: vigorous and simple lines and proportions, expressed with delicate and studied appreciation of every detail. Such is art, and so it has always been: subtle and finely sensitive. The bold, bombastic, too forward and obvious things go as much too far as the weak and vacillating ones fall behind! The man of genius learns to seek that "certain best point" to which Aristotle drew the world's attention, "which," as he put it, "we should always strive to attain, but refrain from surpassing."

There is a third class of building, the ideal type that sustains us all, where art and utility go hand in hand. True, the giant Goliath, "competition" has to be met here, as a rule, but often it is by some youthful David that he is brought to the ground; and we all have hope in a competition, for the judgments nowadays are apt to be fair, and the awards worthy of one's best effort. What an honor to create a building such as this library of Columbia College! or the new Department of Justice in Washington! or a monument such as the one now about to be built to commemorate Lincoln! And how ineradicable is the mistake, when an architect fails to rise to the level of his opportunity. The doctor's mistakes are all underground, but the architect's mistakes live to accuse him to all the world.

Bosworth's Post-1916 Career

Although some of Bosworth's subsequent American commissions were office buildings, like the Ocean Cable Office Building (1916) (since demolished), most were houses, estates, and townhouses, like the houses for William Barclay Parsons (121 East 65th Street) and Philip Gossler (14 East 65th Street) in New York, a mansion for Walter Farwell (1920), and house alterations and a garden for Charles A. Stone, both in the Locust Valley area. Also, Vail, who was a great admirer of Italian art and had traveled extensively through Italy, asked Bosworth in 1916 to design his home in Morristown, New Jersey. The building still exists, but it is now the Morristown Town Hall. It is situated on the side of a steep hill to which, typically Bosworthian, it is connected by a series of terraces. The façade of the topmost level of the building has an elegant tripartite loggia overlooking a garden (the long reflecting pool was a later addition) modeled on the so-called Casino in the gardens of the sixteenth-century Farnese Palace in Caprarola, north of Rome.

From 1920 to 1922, Bosworth served on the New York Fine Arts Commission, which reviewed projects for the city, and in 1920 he authored a small, exquisite monograph, the publication of which was paid for by Rockefeller, on the Altoviti Aphrodite sculpture, purchased by Rockefeller and attributed, mistakenly as it turned out, to Praxiteles. Bosworth also designed extensive gardens for the house of Samuel Untermeyer, a famous lawyer, in Yonkers, New York, and Martson Hall at Brown University (1925–1926) in Providence, Rhode Island. In 1925, he designed the aforementioned Egyptian Museum for Cairo.[1]

In 1921, Bosworth built his own house, having acquired a property in Long Island next to Stone's. The house, built on the foundation of an old farmhouse, has very little in common with other neoclassic edifices of that era, even those Bosworth had designed for his own clients. The façade, with its flat pilasters and unadorned surfaces, is based on a fifteenth-century Italian church type that one finds in Rome, such as S. Maria del Popolo (1472–1480) and S. Pietro in Montorio (1483). The proportions of Bosworth's façade are beautifully worked out with the façade divided by a string course into a primary zone and a windowless attic zone, the central element of which is a rondel. The whole is crowned by an elegant, relatively flat pediment that attests to Bosworth's undogmatic approach; the pediment that defines the roof is slightly larger than the underlying pilasters so that the edges actually spring free from the entablature. The interior plan of the house is asymmetrical, consisting of a complex set of interconnected spaces but with a sight axis that goes straight through the building on both the first and second floors.

The third floor housed a studio with clerestory illumination on the sides. Like both the Scarborough School and the Farwell House, Bosworth hid the bulk of the upper floor behind the front parapet. Behind the house, leading away from it, was a long *percée,* or alley, 100 feet wide and 1,000 feet long, bordered by dogwoods and cedars. For the sculpture program, Bosworth called in some IOUs, in particular one from the noted French-American sculptor Gaston Lachaise (1882–1935), whom Bosworth also had brought in for the finishing touches on the AT&T building. Lachaise designed four bas-relief panels for the parapet level that were based on the theme of the four seasons.

Gradually, however, Bosworth's American career, promising as it was, came to an end, and his life took a different turn. Rockefeller, traveling in France in 1922, was appalled at the dire condition of French monuments and set up a fund in 1924 to pay for the restoration of the châteaux of Versailles and Fontainebleau. Bosworth, who possibly drew Rockefeller's attention to this need himself, was put in charge of the project. He also took over the restoration of the Cathedral of Rheims, and in 1935, he founded the University Club of Paris. In 1933, he designed the American Student Social Center for the American Cathedral Church of the Holy Trinity in Paris. The building adjoins the Chateaubriand and is in a Romanesque style. In 1934, he supervised the restoration of Queen Marie Antoinette's Trianon cottage near Versailles. Although Rockefeller's project ended in 1936, Bosworth remained in his adopted country in semiretirement, building a house for himself and his family, Villa Marietta, in Vaucresson (1935–1936).

During World War II, Bosworth was chairman of the Paris committee of the American Volunteer Ambulance Corps. In 1945, he was named associate member of the École des Beaux-Arts. In 1949, he headed a fund drive for restoration of Vimoutiers in Normandy, which had been destroyed by error in a World War II bombing raid. These efforts earned him considerable recognition in France.

Being much honored, he nevertheless retained his natural modesty. When, at age 96, he attended a luncheon of France's five great learned academies as a member of the Institute of France, he mentioned to an officer that he had an appointment elsewhere but did not dare to leave. The officer brought this to the attention of the assembly. The diners, 100 of France's most distinguished scholars, stood up as one man. Mr. Bosworth rose, in happy embarrassment, so it was reported, and, gripping his cane, strode erectly out.[2]

To the end, Bosworth lamented the arrival of functionalist architecture and its engineering mentality. A few years before his death, he wrote a tongue-in-cheek "hymn" for "Old architects, still inspired by Greek Beauty":

> *Mine eyes have seen with sadness*
> *   All this "cutting out of Art";*
> *They have ceased to teach young students*
> *   To make Beauty, play chief part*
> *   "As we go marching on."*
> *But we who know the laws of beauty*
> *   That one very rarely knows,*
> *Can find them spread before us*
> *   When we study a full-blown Rose*
> *   "Glory, glory Halla-lu-a*
> *   As we go marching on."*

W. W. BOSWORTH (1962)

Notes

chapter 1

The Changing Identity of MIT: Why the Move?

1 For a full discussion of the early planning and creation of the Institute, see Prescott, pp. 21–32.

2 Preston graduated from Harvard College and received his early training in the office of his father, who was also an architect. Later he studied at the École des Beaux-Arts in Paris. Besides these two buildings, he also designed the State Charitable Mechanic's Association Building, and he went on to have a flourishing career in Boston, designing both public and private buildings. For a discussion of the history of Copley Square see Douglass Shand-Tucci, *The Gods of Copley Square: The Dawn of the Modern American Experience, 1860–1965* (New York: St. Martin's Press, forthcoming 2005).

3 When the Natural History Museum moved to its new building on the Charles River Dam, the name of the organization was changed to the Museum of Science. The original building still stands and is currently a clothing store. The Rogers Building and the Walker building, however, were torn down in 1939 to make way for the New England Mutual Life Insurance Co. building. Originally, the MIT museum, with its industry and art exhibits, was meant to serve as a teaching museum. There are two façade studies for the Rogers Building that show the change from a three-story to a four-story structure, which led the way to the five-story building that was ultimately constructed. Bainbridge Bunting has argued that the MIT building is a reworking of the pavilion motif used in the Place de la Concorde in Paris. See Bunting, pp. 76–77. I suggest that Preston's design was influenced by the works of Robert Adam. The first façade is reminiscent of the Shelburne House (1762–1768) or the Kenwood House (1767–1769), whereas the second seems to be influenced by the south façade of Adam's Kedleston Hall (1760).

4 Apsley House was originally designed and built by Robert Adam (1771–1778) with a plain brick façade. The duke purchased the house in 1817 and made it his London home after a military career in India, Portugal, and Spain, which culminated in his victory over Napoleon at Waterloo in 1815. He had the house enlarged by Wyatt in 1828.

5 The Women's Laboratory was founded in 1876 by Ellen Swallow Richards to give women laboratory training in chemistry. It was a nondegree program until 1883, when women could become degree candidates.

6 A detachment of students was sent to Philadelphia, with MIT's president John D. Runkle himself spending a good deal of time studying the technical and educational exhibits. Runkle brought back to Boston samples of work done by Russian students, including the plans for the shops in which the work was done. The 125' x 40' "Annex" was modeled on one of those plans. See Prescott, pp. 97–98. See also John D. Runkle, *Proceedings of the Brookline Historical Society for 1953*, p. 12 [File "John D. Runkle, Correspondence," MIT Museum].

7 See Prescott, p. 98, and H. W. Tyler, "John D. Runkle, 1822–1902," p. 2022 [File "John D. Runkle, Correspondence," MIT Museum].

8 Fehmer, who immigrated to the United States as a young man, became a member of the Boston Society of Architects in 1870. In 1882, Fehmer made a name for himself by building the Boston residence of Oliver Ames. He also designed the Creighton Hotel (1878) and other buildings in Boston. Oliver Ames (1831–1895) served as a lieutenant colonel in the Massachusetts Militia prior to the Civil War, during which he managed the family's manufacturing operations. He was made president of several banks, railroads, and other companies. He was elected to the Senate, serving from 1881 until 1883, and was lieutenant governor from 1883 until his election as governor in 1887. Ames advocated banking reforms and public funding of education. After three terms as governor, Ames declined to run for a fourth term and returned to family and business concerns.

9 Letter by Bosworth to Miss Schillaber, April 19, 1954, p. 3 [MC 612, Box #77, 93 (Correspondence, Fassett with Bosworth), MIT Archives].

10 Rogers used the Polytechnical Institute at Karlsruhe as a model. See Prescott, p. 43.

11 It was originally a roller-skating rink that had been redesigned by Ralph Adams Cram. See also "A General Meeting Place," *The Technique* 23 (1909), pp. 334–338.

12 See Prescott, p. 43.

13 Two of the proposed buildings did get built. See Floyd, pp. 402–403.

14 Ibid., p. 270. For a biography of Vail, see Albert B. Paine, *Theodore N. Vail: A Life* (New York: Harper Publishers, 1929).

15 "Tech Receives Important Gift," *The Technology Review* 15/3 (March 1913), p. 158. It was actually the Edward Dering Library that Vail donated. It consisted of more than 18,000 volumes. See Ruth M. Lane, "The Vail Library at Technology," *The Tech-Engineering News: The Professional Journal of the Undergraduates of the Massachusetts Institute of Technology* 4/6 (December 1923), pp. 201, 236–246. Vail purchased the George Edward Dering library sight unseen at the suggestion of a bookseller in London at the time of Dering's death in 1913. Dering was a well-known eccentric, inventor, and thinker who, over the course of his lifetime, collected virtually every publication he ever encountered on the subject of electricity.

16 "Hearing Before Joint Committee on Education," *The Technology Review* 13/2 (February 1911), p. 112.

17 Richard Maclaurin, "University and Industries," *Journal of Industrial and Engineering Chemistry* 8/1 (1916), p. 59 [Richard C. Maclaurin Papers 1892–1908, Box #6, Reprint p. 3, MIT Archives].

18 In 1902, three cousins, T. Coleman and Pierre S. and Alfred I. du Pont, purchased the Du Pont Company and molded it into a broad, science-based chemical company. The trio modernized the company's management, built scientific research labs, and expanded into and marketed new products such as paints, plastics, and dyes, technologies that were based on the same raw materials and by-products of the explosives business they knew so well. In 1913, Coleman du Pont announced plans for the forty-story, $30 million Equitable Building at 120 Broadway, with 2,300 offices for 15,000 people. It was finished in 1915. In that year Coleman relinquished the presidency, and Pierre purchased his shares through the newly formed DuPont Securities Company. Coleman went on to become an investor and later a Republican United States senator for Delaware.

19 Theodore H. Skinner graduated in 1892 and was the more senior of the pair. William P. Rand, a specialist in construction technology, graduated in 1900. After graduating, Skinner worked for McKim, Mead, and White, and was their job captain for the University of Virginia buildings in 1898. He eventually moved to Florida, specializing in houses and office buildings. The engineer of the building, as will be discussed later, was Frank B. Gilbreth.

20 "Process of Construction of the Augustus Lowell Laboratory of Electrical Engineering for the Massachusetts Institute of Technology," 1902 [MIT Boston Campus—Lowell Building: MIT Museum]. Also see Gilbreth's books. For the famous story of life in the Gilbreth household, see Gilbreth Jr. and Carey.

chapter 2   President Maclaurin and the New Site

1 In 1902 Guy Lowell chaired a thesis project in Landscape Architecture by A. R. Nichols that investigated redesigning the area around the Rogers Building for an expanded MIT campus. See *Architectural Annual of the Massachusetts Institute of Technology, 1901-1902* (Boston: Architectural Society, 1902), p. 61.

2 "Shall the Institute Remove from Its Present Site," *The Technology Review* 4/3 (July 1902), pp. 307-316.

3 Letter to Dr. Pritchett, June 17, 1903 [MIT, Boston Campus—General Proposals for Expansion: MIT Museum]. Pritchett was MIT president from 1900 until 1907.

4 In 1907, after returning to Boston from the Telephone Company, Fish resumed practice in the firm of Fish, Richardson, Herrick & Neave, with offices in Boston and New York.

5 Letter to Frederick W. Taylor, November 6, 1914, p. 2 [Freeman, Box #41, MIT Archives].

6 He was born in Edinburgh, Scotland, in 1870, but spent his boyhood in New Zealand. In 1892, he entered the University of Cambridge and studied mathematics and later law. In 1898, he became a mathematics professor at the University of New Zealand and then Dean of Law in 1903. In 1907, he took an appointment as chair of the Department of Mathematical Physics at the University of Columbia and later became head of the department.

7 Compare Henry S. Pritchett, "Shall the University Become a Business Corporation?," *The Atlantic Monthly* 46 (September 1905), pp. 289-299 with Richard Maclaurin, "Darwin at an American University," *The Atlantic Monthly* 58 (September 1905), pp. 192-198.

8 *Technique 1912* [1911], p. 380.

9 Maclaurin, "Darwin at an American University," p. 198.

10 "The Institute in Retrospect and Prospect," *The Technology Review* 15/2 (February 1913), p. 141.

11 Maclaurin, "University and Industries," *Journal of Industrial and Engineering Chemistry* 8/1 (1916), p. 59 [Richard C. Maclaurin Papers 1892-1908, Box #6, Reprint p. 5, 4, MIT Archives].

12 *The Technology Review* 13/4 (April 1911), p. 227.

13 In a letter to Maclaurin, Carnegie writes, "If I mistake not, I am part owner of that ground that my friend Lee Higginson and some of us purchased to unite the two institutions, which should be done." See Prescott, p. 250.

14 Ibid., p. 245. See also "Future Relations with Harvard," *The Technology Review* 15/1

(January 1913), pp. 1–6. Harvard pressed its case by awarding Maclaurin an honorary doctorate in 1910, but when Maclaurin continued to resist, Harvard sent him a letter stating in no uncertain terms that the university was "strongly of the opinion that it would be a very serious peril to both institutions to have the Institute of Technology establish itself in Cambridge." See Pearson, pp. 105–106.

15 "Alumni Preparing for a Supreme Effort," *The Technology Review* 14/3 (March 1912), p. 153.

16 The rest of the amount was contributed by various friends and alumni.

17 According to Maclaurin, "Research work in technical chemistry and physical chemistry will most likely be the first [building to be] given a place on the new site." "Cambridge Removes the Last Obstacle," *The Technology Review* 14/1 (January 1912), p. 3.

18 "The Growing Influence of the Alumni," *The Technology Review* 15/2 (February 1913), p. 151, and "Alumni Preparing for a Supreme Effort," *The Technology Review* 14/3 (March 1912), p. 154.

chapter 3

The First Design of Stephen Child

1 There are numerous other possibilities, but I base my conjecture not on the design itself, but on the style of the trees. They are very similar to those in the firm's 1887 drawing of Stanford University. The way trees are drawn tends to be distinctive to a renderer's style.

2 The aerial perspective was published in the article "Hearing Before Joint Committee on Education," *The Technology Review* 13/2 (February 1911), p. 113. *The Technique* 26 (1912), pp. 50–52, published the perspectives of both projects. The yearbook, it should be noted, was published to appear in 1912 and thus reflects the state of the designs in 1911 before the land was purchased. Neither plan is for the Cambridge site as both show a landscape of farms and trees.

3 See Bunting, *Harvard*, p. 83.

4 "A Report on a Proposed Development of The New Technology at Cambridge, Massachusetts by Stephen Child '88: Landscape Architect—Consulting Engineer. Boston, Mass.—Santa Barbara, Cal. Submitted to President Richard C. Maclaurin, December 30, 1911" [Freeman, Box #41, MIT Archives].

5 At MIT he had planned to specialize in civic engineering, but he shifted to landscape design, starting his own practice in 1903.

chapter 4

Désiré Despradelle's Alternative

1 Constant Antoine Désiré Despradelle arrived in Boston from Paris in 1893. He had studied at the École des Beaux-Arts, in the course of which he received several prizes. At MIT he transplanted certain key aspects of the Beaux-Arts system of atelier teaching to the Department of Architecture. One of his students, Guy Lowell, went on to design the Museum of Fine Arts in Boston. A visit to the 1893 World's Columbian Exposition in Chicago inspired him to create a "Beacon of Progress" in the form of a towering 1,500-foot monument dedicated to the American nation. The project was awarded a gold medal and exhibited at the 1900 Paris Salon. Had he found sufficient backing for his design, the resulting structure would have been by far the tallest manmade object in the world. Plans called for a 1,500-foot stone tower in Jackson Park, Chicago, on the site of the 1893 Chicago World's Fair, which had celebrated technological progress. Despradelle also entered the local Boston debate over how best to reconfigure Copley Square. In 1898, he was in California to make a proposal for the proposed University of California at Berkeley. In Boston, he designed the Berkeley Building (1905), a complex of factory and warehouse buildings at Causeway and North Washington Streets (1906–1912), and the Peter Bent Brigham Hospital, now Brigham and Women's Hospital, which opened after his death.

2 These were designed with his partner Stephen Russel H. Codman (1867–1944). Codman attended Harvard University and studied for one year at MIT. He lived in Paris between 1889 and 1893, and upon his return set up a practice in Boston.

3 The first plan is published in *The Technology Review* 13/5 (May 1911), p. 311. The last one is published in *The Technology Review* 13/9 (December 1911), p. 619.

A Third Design: Ralph Adams Cram's?

chapter 5

1 *The Technology Review* 14/1 (January 1912), p. 77.

2 Cram (1863–1942) held his first appointment at MIT beginning in 1914. In 1916, he became chairman of the Department of Architecture. He resigned in 1919 in order to dedicate himself to his practice.

3 See Haglund, pp. 188–189.

4 "To Build an Island in the Charles for the Tech," *The Technology Review* 13/2 (February 1911), p. 145.

5 See Haglund, p. 189.

6 "Site Chosen for the Institute," *The Technology Review* 13/8 (November 1911), p. 484.

The Eastman Millions

chapter 6

1 Eastman admired MIT because his two top assistants, Frank Lovejoy and Darragh de Lancey, were graduates of the school. He held a meeting with Richard Cockburn Maclaurin, the president of MIT, at the Hotel Belmont in New York on March 5. To preserve his desire for anonymity, he was called Mr. Smith. Eastman was one of the great philanthropists of his age. He also gifted the University of Rochester $35.5 million over the years before his death and an additional $19 million from his estate. Maclaurin's biographer stated that Frank Greenleaf Pearson and Maclaurin had spent a whole evening with Eastman. Finally, after hearing what they had to say, Eastman asked, "What sum would be needed?" "Two and a half million," Maclaurin replied. Eastman told him, "I shall send you a draft for that amount." Maclaurin had considered calling Eastman an "anonymous giver" but later concluded that it was too clumsy to be used daily. So he decided on the name "Mr. Smith," which stuck. Maclaurin revealed that Eastman was Mr. Smith in his final speech before his death in 1919. He was then only fifty years old. See Pearson, pp. 126–127, and Prescott, pp. 262–264.

chapter 7   Freeman to the Rescue

1 According to Maclaurin, "Research work in technical chemistry and physical chemistry will most likely be the first given a place on the new site." "Cambridge Removes the Last Obstacle," *The Technology Review* 14/1 (January 1912), p. 3.

2 This episode is described in Haglund, pp. 174–176.

3 Letter to S. P. Eastman, April 27, 1912 [Freeman, Box #41, MIT Archives].

4 "Technology Gets $2,500,000 Gift," *Providence Journal* (March 14, 1912) [Freeman, Box #41, MIT Archives].

5 It is interesting to compare the list in Child's report with Freeman's. See John R. Freeman, "Notes on 'Study No. 7' for New Technology" [Freeman, MC 51, Box #42, MIT Archives].

6 "'Efficiency' Key-Note of Alumni Banquet," *The Technology Review* 13/2 (February 1911), pp. 122–124.

7 See Schachter, p. 28.

8 Freeman describes Taylor as "my old friend." "Freeman autobiography," p. 313 [John R. Freeman File, MIT Museum]. See, for example, pp. 15–18, where he describes his parents and upbringing.

9 "Technology Its Own Architect," *The Technology Review* 14/8 (November 1912), p. 539. The author is not given, but it is clearly written by or conceived by Freeman.

10 Ibid.

11 Schachter, p. 51.

12 "Dr. Maclaurin on Technology Efficiency," *The Technology Review* 13/2 (February 1911), pp. 136–144.

13 Richard Maclaurin, "University and Industries," *Journal of Industrial and Engineering Chemistry* 8/1 (1916), p. 59 [Richard C. Maclaurin Papers 1892–1908, Box #6, Reprint p. 4, MIT Archives].

14 "Dr. Maclaurin on Technology Efficiency," p. 137.

15 See Roy McLennan, the Career of Richard C. McClaurin [*sic*], Vol. II—The Last Years (Working Paper of the Alfred P. Sloan School of Management #748-75, pp. 10–11 [File "Richard C. Maclaurin, Correspondence," The MIT Museum].

16 "Planning the New Technology, Study No. 7," p. 10 [Freeman, Box #41, MIT Archives].

chapter 8   "Study No. 7"

1 MIT Annual Report of the President to the Corporation, December 11, 1912.

2 John R. Freeman, "Notes on 'Study No. 7' for New Technology" [Freeman, MC 51, Box #42, MIT Archives].

3 Freeman, "Notes," p. 10.

4 Freeman, "Notes," p. 12.

5 Letter to Sanford E. Thompson, December 1, 1912, p. 3 [Freeman, Box #41, MIT Archives].

6 Freeman, "Notes," p. 9.

7 Albert P. Carman, "The Design of a Physical Laboratory," *The Brickbuilder* 20/12 (December 1911), pp. 257–260.

8 "Present Day Factory Construction," *The American Architect and Building News* 49/1851 (June 14, 1911).

9 "The Country Life Press," *The American Architect and Building News* 49/1851 (June 14, 1911), plates not numbered. The building was designed by Henry P. Kirby and John J. Petit.

10 *American Architect and Building News* 99/1851 (June 14, 1911), p. 214. For further discussion, see Banham. See also "Recent Developments in Factory Lighting," *The American Architect* 48/1804 (July 20, 1910), p. 24.

11 "Present Day Factory Construction," *The American Architect* 99/1851 (June 14, 1911), p. 214.

chapter 9   Selection of Cass Gilbert

1 Letter by Freeman to Sanford E. Thompson (December 31, 1912) [Freeman, Box#41, MIT Archives].

2 "Technology Is Its Own Architect," *The Technology Review* 14/8 (November 1912), p. 539. There is no author of the piece, but it is clearly related to Freeman's goals.

3 "Features of the Mass Meeting," *The Technology Review* 15 (February 13, 1913), p. 134.

4 "Growing Influence of the Alumni," *The Technology Review* 15 (February 13, 1913), pp. 151–152.

5 The building on Tremont Street and Pemberton Square was demolished in 1968. Gilbert also built the Brazer Building (1896) on State and Devonshire Streets.

6 "New York's Successful Banquet, Thomas A. Edison guest of the Club—Dr. Maclaurin, Cass Gilbert and Gelett Burgess among the speakers," *The Technology Review* 14/2 (February 1912), pp. 133–134. On February 2, 1913, Gilbert was featured on the cover page of the *Boston Sunday Post,* Second Feature Section, which was entitled "Boston Tech Men Doing the Big Things of the World Today." See also "To Hold Alumni Dinner," *The Technology Review* 14/8 (November 1912), p. 522.

7 This quotation is taken from notes made by Gail Fenske, who is currently writing a book called *Gilbert and the Woolworth Building.* The original letter is currently slated for restoration but is, according to the archivist of the New-York Historical Society, off limits to further study for an indefinite period of time. See "Letter, March 1, 1913 to Mr. Tracy Lyon," Cass Gilbert Collection, New-York Historical Society, Personal Letterbooks, Correspondence. My thanks to Fenske for access to her notes.

8 Albert Kahn to Freeman, dated 1/24/1913 [Freeman, Box #41, "MIT Correspondence," MIT Archives].

9 "Minutes of the Executive Committee," January 27, 1913 [folder: May 13, 1912–May 19, 1913].

10 Telegram dated February 5, 1913, from Freeman to Richard C. Maclaurin [Freeman File, MIT Museum].

11 Letter by Newell to Charles A. Stone, February 4, 1913 [Freeman, Box #41, "MIT Correspondence," February 1913, MIT Archives]. Stone (1867–1941) was born and raised in Newton, Massachusetts. After his graduation from MIT in 1888, he achieved notable success with his partner Edwin S. Webster in the field of electrical engineering, managing all types of public utilities, which drew them into the banking and investment businesses. They were soon involved in large construction projects and became one of the largest construction firms in the United States. Newell, who graduated in 1885, became the director in 1907 and was in charge of numerous government projects such as dams, tunnels, bridges, and reservoirs. He was also an active member in numerous scientific organizations. He had been a term member of MIT's corporation from 1906 to 1909.

chapter 10

William Welles Bosworth Becomes a Candidate

1 John Rockefeller Sr. purchased the property at Pocantico Hills in 1893, together with an architecturally undistinguished Victorian frame house. The new house in a French villa style was begun in 1906 and completed in 1913 and is credited to the architects William Adams Delano and Chester Holmes Aldrich. Bosworth was brought in for the gardens in 1907. For a study of Bosworth's designs, see S. Quentin Jacobs, *William Welles Bosworth: Major Works* (Master's Thesis, Columbia University, 1988), pp. 44–66. See also Pierson.

2 See Pierson, p. 54.

chapter 11

Bosworth's Early Architectural Training

1 During Bosworth's lifetime, the most substantive pieces on his life and work were "The Garden at Pocantico Hills, Estate of John D. Rockefeller Esq.," *The American Architect* 49/1828 (January 4, 1911), pp. 1–12 (authored by Bosworth); "The Scarboro-on-Hudson School," *American Architect* 115/2258 (April 2, 1919), pp. 476–480; "The Relation of Classic Example to Architectural Design, with Particular Reference to the Work of Welles Bosworth," *American Architect* 122/2397 (July 5, 1920), pp. 1–12, 20–21 (authored by Bosworth); and "Master Draftsman, Welles Bosworth," *Pencil Points* 6 (January 1925), pp. 59–64. Bosworth also wrote "Some Observations on Architectural Disymmetry," *American Architect* 48/1813 (September 21, 1910), pp. 93–98; "Letters to C.R.E. Architect, About a Little Journey in the Oise Valley," *American Architect* 48/1823 (November 30, 1910), pp. 177–179; "Mens Sana in Corpore Sano," *The Architectural Record* 30/2 (August 1911), pp. 150–159; and "I Knew H. H. Richardson," *Journal of the American Institute of Architects* (September 1951), pp. 115–126.

2 While still a student, he attracted the attention of the renowned architect Henry Hobson Richardson, designer of Boston's famous Trinity Church. Bosworth was set to work on the presentation drawings and furniture designs for Richardson's Pittsburgh Court House project. He designed corbels, using the faces of his friends for models. After Richardson's death in 1886, the firm passed into the hands of Charles A. Coolidge and George Shepley, who kept Bosworth in their employ, sending him to the Brookline offices of Frederick Law Olmsted to help out with the drawings that were part of Olmsted's competition entry for the design of Stanford University. There he met and became friends with Thomas Hastings, one of Richardson's draftsmen. Hastings would later hire Bosworth for his firm, Carrère and Hastings.

3 Hampton Normal and Agricultural Institute was established in 1868 by General Samuel Chapman Armstrong (1839–1893). It was reorganized in the 1920s and is now Hampton College. Although Bosworth would often claim that he was responsible for several buildings there, in reality his contribution was relatively minor and is limited to the Science and Treasury buildings (1889). The two buildings were wood-frame, shingled structures. See *Southern Workman and Hampton School Record* 18/2 (February 1889), p. 12, which references the construction of the building.

4 According to Bosworth, "I come from a long line of Puritan preachers on one side of the house and from a long line of liberal minded New York Dutch on the other, but devout Christians. My mother's grand-father, Wyant van Zandt, gave an Episcopal Church to the town of Douglastown, on Long Island, and is buried in the family vault under the stone pavement at the entrance to Trinity Church at the head of Wall Street" [Bosworth, "Letter to F. G. Fassett Junior," May 7, 1953, MC 162, Box #77, 93, Correspondence Fassett with Bosworth, MIT Archives].

5 This view was published in *American Architect* 22/2399 (August 2, 1922), p. 103.

6 As was typical, students of the Beaux-Arts supplemented their studies by working in the ateliers of their teachers. Bosworth is known to have worked in the atelier of François Benjamin Chaussemiche, but he worked the longest at the atelier of Gaston Redon (1853–1921), the architect responsible for restoration work at Versailles. Bosworth later inherited his position.

7 For the plan, see "The Work of Messrs. Carrère and Hastings," *The Architectural Record* 27/1 (January 1910), p. 68.

8 He also designed three small buildings for the Exhibition, including the Forestry Building, a one-story structure with a low-gabled roof made entirely of logs. Bosworth's work on the layout of the 1901 Pan American Exhibition got him his next set of commissions, a house for Frederick de Peyster Townsend, who was involved in the planning of the Exhibition, and another, more important one, for John C. Milburn, president of the Exhibition Corporation (1907). Bosworth also designed a clubhouse for the Mohawk Golf Club in Schenectady, N.Y. (1903), and the New York Magdalen Benevolent Society Asylum in New York City (1904).

9 In that year, Bosworth was hired by the design firm Cram, Goodhue, and Ferguson to make the presentation drawings for their competition entry for West Point Military Academy. The firm rarely used perspectives for their presentation drawings and was afraid that this inexperience would show. As Cram recalled, they won the competition to no small degree because of Bosworth's skill.

chapter 12   Vanderlip, Vail, and Bosworth

1 S. Quentin Jacobs, *William Welles Bosworth: Major Works* (Master's Thesis, Columbia University, 1988), p. 162. This work also contains an excellently researched list of Bosworth's built and unbuilt projects.

2 Barker, the founder of the Washington Insurance Company, served on the Board of Fellows of Brown University, and filled numerous important offices in the state. He was the father of Governor Charles Jackson of Rhode Island. He was educated at the Friends' School in Providence, the Englewood Military Academy at Perth Amboy, N.J., and the Rensselear Institute in Troy, N.Y. He was appointed judge advocate of the First Brigade, Rhode Island Militia, by General Burnside when he was only eighteen years old and served on Burnside's staff. His wife, Eliza Harris Lawton, was keenly interested in educational affairs and became a member of the corporation of the Woman's College at Brown University. They called their house on Narragansett Bay "The Outlook."

3 Published in *American Architect and Building News* 78/1400 (October 25, 1902), p. 31.

4 Published in *Architectural Record* 24 (July 1908), pp. 49–52.

5 Valentine Everit Macy (1871–1930), a noted philanthropist and public official, was born in New York City. His grandfather Josiah Jr. and his father William H. had established the firm of Josiah Macy & Son in New York in 1828. When Josiah Jr. died in 1876, he left a large estate. Valentine entered the Columbia University College of Architecture and received his degree in 1893, but he was never active professionally. For many years he was chiefly occupied with the care of his estate, giving much time to public causes, notably the Teachers College of Columbia University, the Metropolitan Museum of Art, and the National Child Labor Committee. The family had several connections to Standard Oil and the Rockefellers.

6 Initially, the Vanderlips had been interested in the Montessori system, but they became disillusioned with it and decided to set up their own school, with an emphasis on workshop activity and theater. Their ideas were consistent with the newly developing pedagogy of the time. New York City was itself undergoing a school building boom with some schools, like the Manhattan Trade School for Girls (1902), established under the auspices of New York's growing philanthropic movement. The Scarborough school, however, was to combine the idea of healthy work with theater, from which the young scions were to perfect social skills and speech.

7 For a contemporary description, see "The Scarboro-on-Hudson School," *American Architect* 95/2258 (April 2, 1919), pp. 476–480.

8 In 1907, the New York State Board of Charities cited the need for a facility to care for the "feeble-minded and epileptics." The state purchased 2,000 acres of rolling farm country in Thiels (Rockland County, New York) to build the facility. In 1909, the facility was named Letchworth Village in honor of William Pryor Letchworth (1823–1910), a noted philanthropist, humanitarian, and advocate for the project. Letchworth's vision differed from the standard custodial-type of institutions that were built during the nineteenth century. He wanted a facility that approximated a "village" life and that would provide education, training, and vocations to children and adults with mental retardation and developmental disabilities. Letchworth's farms were worked by those residing at the facility. The farm remained active until the early 1960s. See *Life at Letchworth Village,* "The Fourth Annual Report of the Board of Visitors for the Fiscal Year Ended March 31, 1948" (State of New York: Department of Mental Hygiene, 1948), in which Bosworth writes, "What Stands Out in My Mind as I Think of Letchworth Village," pp. 111–112.

9 Bosworth, "What Stands Out in My Mind as I Think of Letchworth Village," *Life at Letchworth Village,* p. 112.

10 It is located on 195 Broadway. By the late 1870s, Western Union, led by William H. Vanderbilt, had become the leading force in telegraphy. The sight of a uniformed Western Union messenger boy was familiar in small towns and big cities all over the country. In 1908, AT&T, originally founded by Bell, gained control of Western Union. This proved beneficial to Western Union, because the companies were able to share lines when needed, and it became possible to order telegrams by telephone. In 1913, however, as part of a move to prevent the government from invoking antitrust laws, AT&T divested itself from Western Union. From 1885 to 1910, AT&T was headquartered at 125 Milk Street in Boston. The New York building was built in three sections. The first was begun in 1913 in the area now occupied by the employment office. The second extended along Dey Street about two-thirds of the distance between Broadway and Church Street. The third section (1921–1924) replaced two buildings then at the corner of Broadway and Fulton Street and was originally known as 205 Broadway. The statue now stands in the lobby of the AT&T building at 550 Madison Avenue.

The building's original shape was an odd one, since the corner property had not yet been purchased. As a result, the bulk of the property was a narrow rectangle with a small sliver of land providing the building's entrance from Fulton Street. Bosworth took advantage of this unusual arrangement by extending that sliver into a veritable campanile, at the top of which was a stepped pyramidal structure modeled on the Mausoleum of Halicarnassus, which had just recently been excavated and studied. See, for example, A. L. Frothingham, "Greek Architects," *The Architectural Record* 23/2 (February 1908), pp. 81–96. At its summit was Evelyn Beatrice Longman's sculpture *The Genius of Telegraphy,* later renamed *The Spirit of Communication.* Bosworth drew a beautiful rendering that was later published in *L'architecture aux États-Unis* (1920) by Jacques Greber, a Parisian designer whom Bosworth would later call in to help in the designing of MIT's 77 Massachusetts Avenue entrance, and who would develop a career of his own in the United States and Canada.

Eventually, the corner site of the block was purchased, and Bosworth was asked to finish the building, which he did by expanding the hypostyle hall and adding squash courts and a sunbathing deck on the roof. Paul Manship, who was to become friends with Bosworth, designed the panels over the Broadway entrances, the plaque of Alexander Graham Bell, and the turbaned Asian maidens supporting the drinking fountains.

11 "The Relation of Classic Example to Architectural Design," *The American Architect* 122/2397 (July 5, 1922), p. 6. An author is not given, but it is most probably Bosworth.

12 Ibid.

13 Ibid., pp. 1–2.

chapter 13

Bosworth Gets the Nod

1 "The Growing Influence of the Alumni: Address of President Maclaurin at the Mass Meeting of Technology Clubs, the Plaza, New York City, January 17," *The Technology Review* 15 (1913), pp. 150–152.

2 "Statement with Reference to Bosworth," p. 3 [Freeman, Box #41, Correspondence January 1913–February 1913, MIT Archives]. This letter summarizes the contents of the recommendation letters. It is not dated, but a letter by Maclaurin dated February 17, 1913, makes reference to it.

3 Ibid.

4 He was elected in March 1916, just a month before the grand opening.

5 Letter by Bosworth to Freeman, February 17, 1913 [Freeman File, MIT Museum].

6 Letter by Maclaurin to Freeman, February 17, 1913 [Freeman, Box #41, MIT Archives].

7 Letter by Freeman to Frederick W. Taylor, Consulting Engineer, November 6, 1914 [Freeman, Box #41, MIT Archives].

8 Letter by Freeman to M. L. Cooke (Director of Public Works, Philadelphia, Pennsylvania), October 22, 1914 [Freeman, Box #41, MIT Archives].

9 Letter to Frederick W. Taylor, November 6, 1914, p. 2 [Freeman, Box #41, MIT Archives].

10 Letter by Freeman to M. L. Cooke, October 22, 1914 [Freeman, Box #41, MIT Archives].

11 Letter to Walter E. Spear, dated April 1, 1913 [Freeman, Box #41, MIT Correspondence, MIT Archives].

12 Freeman autobiography [John R. Freeman File, MIT Museum].

chapter 14

The Gentleman and the Architect

1 The photograph was taken on January 25, 1915. Vail was staying at the cottage while recuperating from a leg injury. See McCash and McCash. See also Edward Marshall, "What Transcontinental Wireless Phone Means: Theodore N. Vail Discusses Significance of Recent Development in Communication. When Human Voice Was Heard for First Time Across Continent," *New York Times Magazine* (October 17, 1915), p. 9.

2 Letter, William Welles Bosworth to John D. Rockefeller Jr., November 12, 1956, p. 1. Bosworth file (Box #108, B71), Rockefeller Archives Center.

3 Trowbridge graduated from Trinity College in 1883 and from Columbia in 1886. He studied at the Atelier Daumet at the École des Beaux-Arts in Paris and was associated with George B. Post from 1894 to 1898. In 1898 he created the firm of Trowbridge & Livingston. He became a Fellow of the American Institute of Architects in 1906 and was an Associate of the National Academy of Design. He was also a member and for a time president of the New York Architectural League. Work by the firm in New York included Bankers Trust Company, Morgan Building, New York Stock Exchange addition, B. Altman store, the Palace Hotel in San Francisco, and the Mellon National Bank in Pittsburgh. His foreign honors included the Legion of Honor, the Greek Order of the Redeemer, and Grand Commander of the Order of the Crown, Romania.

chapter 15

Bosworth's Designs for MIT

1 Joseph Herendeen Clark, a young designer working for McKim, Mead, and White, was loaned to Bosworth to assist in the design development and to serve as Bosworth's Resident Architect during the period of construction. See "The Autobiography of an Architect" by Joseph Herendeen Clark, Portola Valley, California, 1974 [MIT—Cambridge Campus—Construction, "Joseph Herendeen Clark, Pictures and Autobiography," MIT Museum].

2 William Welles Bosworth, "New Buildings for the Massachusetts Institute of Technology, Cambridge Mass.," *The Architectural Review* 2/9 Old Series, Vol. 19 (September 1913), pp. 239–241 with Plates 63–67. See also "New Technology Plans Announced," *The Technology Review* 15/8 (November 1913), pp. 535–550.

chapter 16

Bosworth-Freeman Synthesis

1 "Stone & Webster to Be Construction Engineers," *The Technology Review* 15/8 (November 1913), p. 549.

2 Letter to M. L. Cooke (Director of Public Works, Philadelphia, Pennsylvania), October 22, 1914, p. 1 [Freeman, Box #41, MIT Archives].

3 Letter to Frederick W. Taylor, November 4, 1914, p. 2 [Freeman, Box #41, MIT Archives]. Another contributing factor was the fact that Harold Eric Kebon, a graduate of the Institute from 1912, was chosen as the local Boston representative of Bosworth. Kebon had been employed by Freeman for the development of Study No. 7 and had traveled across the United States gathering material. See H. E. Kebon, "12 Now in Charge," *The Tech* (November 8, 1913), p. 4.

chapter 17   Between the Lines of Modernity

1 See footnote 4 in chapter 11.
2 Hermann Muthesius, "Das Formproblem im Ingenieurbau," *Jahrbuch des deutschen Werkbundes: Die Kunst in Industrie und Handel* (Jena: Eugen Diederich, 1913), pp. 1–12.

chapter 18   The Grand Opening

1 For a contemporary description, see Robert E. Rogers, "The Pageantry of 1916: An Eyewitness Account," in *The Alumni Association Celebrates the 75th Anniversary of MIT's Move from Boston to Cambridge* (Cambridge: MIT, June 13, 1991).
2 Music was composed by James Ecker; costumes were designed by C. Howard Walker.

chapter 19   The Campus Plan

1 "The Growing Influence of the Alumni," *The Technology Review* 15/2 (February 1913), p. 151, and "Alumni Preparing for a Supreme Effort," *The Technology Review* 14/3 (March 1912), p. 154.

chapter 20   The Dome

1 During World War II, the dome was covered to protect the building from a potential German aerial attack. The insertion of what can only be described as street lamps to illuminate the interior added to its gloom.
2 The design by John Soane for a mausoleum is also remarkably similar in proportion. Bosworth must have felt that this Enlightenment-era neoclassicism was more appropriate to the library than the more austere classicism of the exterior.

chapter 21   The Portico

1 The columns, from the echinus of the capital, including base, are 43 feet high. They are four feet ten inches in diameter. The columns stand out nine inches further from the center than at the sides.
2 Letter by Bosworth to Dean Fassett, January 8, 1963, p. 3 [MC 162, Box #1, MIT Archives].

chapter 23   The Statue of Minerva

1 Letter by Bosworth to Fassett, July 24, 1961 [MC 162, Box #77, 93, MIT Archives]. Fassett came to the Massachusetts Institute of Technology in 1930 as an instructor in the Department of English and History. He was named an assistant professor in 1934 and an associate professor in 1938. He was editor of *The Technology Review* from 1939 to 1945 and then director of publications and public relations at the Carnegie Institute of Washington from 1945 until 1951. He then returned to MIT as director of publications of Technology Press. As dean, he was housemaster of Ashdown from 1965 until 1966.

2 Letter to Lester D. Garner, June 7, 1922 [File, "William Welles Bosworth," The MIT Museum].

3 Stratton, who got his degree in 1926 in electrical engineering from MIT, served as the Institute's eleventh president from 1959 until 1966. He had joined the faculty of MIT as an assistant professor in the Department of Electrical Engineering in 1928. In 1930 he transferred to the Department of Physics. A trustee of the Ford Foundation from 1955 to 1971, he served as its chairman from 1966 to 1971. In 1967, President Lyndon B. Johnson appointed him chairman of the Commission on Marine Science, Engineering and Resources.

4 Letter by Bosworth to Fassett, July 24, 1961 [MC 162, Box #77, 93, MIT Archives].

5 Ibid.

6 Letter by Stratton to Fassett, December 28, 1962 [MC 162, Box #77, 93, MIT Archives].

chapter 24   The Genesis of MIT's Ionic Capitals

1 The only difference is that the overall design of the MIT bases is slightly more taut, which I believe was necessary given the enormity of the columns, which are twice as high as those on the Erechtheion.

2 Bosworth would have gotten the drawings from Joseph Durm's recently published book *Die Baukunst der Griechen* (Leipzig: Kröner, 1882, 1910). The garlands over the columns are taken from the monument of Trafyllus in Athens.

chapter 25   Walker Memorial, the Dormitories, and the President's House

1 Alfred E. Burton, "From the Faculty Point of View," *The Technology Review* 15/1 (January 1913), p. 11.

2 In 1923, Edwin Howland Blashfield, a graduate of MIT from 1869, began to paint the murals on the inside of Walker.

3 See Charles Elling, "The New Buildings at Massachusetts Institute of Technology," *The Architectural Forum* 27/6 (December 1916), pp. 151–154, and H. E. Kebbon, "Student Housing at the Massachusetts Institute of Technology," ibid., pp. 155–158.

chapter 27   77 Massachusetts Avenue Entrance

1 Letter by Bosworth to Miss Schillaber, April 19, 1954, p. 2 [MC 162, Box #77, 93 (Correspondence Fassett with Bosworth), MIT Archives]. In 1920, Greber was

appointed to the faculty of the new Institute of Urbanism in Paris. He was one of the leaders in the reconstruction and expansion of some French cities between World War I and World War II. He created the plans for the cities of Lille in 1923, Belfort in 1925, Marseilles in 1930 to 1937, Abbeville in 1932, Rouen in 1940, and many others. Greber designed two Parisian garden suburbs, along with many gardens and parks. He also did work on the 1937 World's Fair. Throughout his life, he managed to maintain his North American connections. He came to have a reputation as one of France's leading urban designers and an expert on American planning and design.

2 Letter by Bosworth to Miss Schillaber, April 19, 1954, p. 2 [MC 162, Box #77, 93, MIT Archives].

appendix 2

Bosworth's Lecture: "Mens Sana in Corpore Sano"

1 It was published in *The Architectural Record* 30/2 (August 1911), pp. 150–159.
2 Victor Laloux (1850–1937), a noted exponent of the Beaux-Arts style, was the architect of the Parisian train station of Orsay, inaugurated in 1900. He also designed the city halls in Tours and Roubaix and the train station in Tours.

appendix 3

Bosworth's Post-1916 Career

1 For the Cairo project, see Jeffrey Abt, "The Breasted-Rockefeller Egyptian Museum Project: Philanthropy, Cultural Imperialism and National Resistance," *Art History* 19/4 (December 1996), pp. 551–572.
2 John L. Hess, "Welles Bosworth Is Active at 96," *New York Times,* International Edition, June 28, 1996.

Bibliography

Bacon, Mardges. *Ernest Flagg, Beaux-Arts Architect and Urban Reformer.* Cambridge, Mass.: The MIT Press, 1986.

Banham, Reyner. *A Concrete Atlantis, U.S. Industrial Building and European Modern Architecture.* Cambridge, Mass.: The MIT Press, 1986.

Bergdoll, Barry. *Mastering McKim's Plan: Columbia's First Century on Morningside Heights.* New York: Miriam and Ira Wallach Art Gallery, Columbia University, 1997.

The Boston Society of Natural History, 1830–1930. Boston: The Boston Society of Natural History, 1930.

Bunting, Bainbridge. *Harvard, the Architectural History.* Completed and edited by Margaret Henderson Floyd. Cambridge, Mass.: Belknap Press, 1985.

———. *Houses of Boston's Back Bay.* Cambridge, Mass.: Belknap Press, 1967.

Chafee, Richard. *The Architecture of the École des Beaux-Arts.* New York: Museum of Modern Art, 1977.

Cushing, George M., Jr., *Great Buildings of Boston, A Photographic Guide.* New York: Dover Publications, 1982.

Floyd, Margaret Henderson. *Architectural Education and Boston.* Boston: Boston Architectural Center, 1989.

———. *Architecture After Richardson, Regionalism Before Modernism—Longfellow, Alden and Harlow in Boston and Pittsburgh.* Chicago: The University of Chicago Press, 1994.

Gilbreth, Frank Bunker. *Bricklaying System.* New York: M. C. Clark, 1909.

———. *Concrete System.* New York: The Engineering News Publishing Company, 1908.

———. *Field System.* New York: M. C. Clark, 1908.

Gilbreth, Frank B., Jr., and Ernestine Gilbreth Carey. *Cheaper by the Dozen.* New York: T. Y. Crowell Co., 1948.

Grossman, Elizabeth G. *The Civic Architecture of Paul Cret.* New York: Cambridge University Press, 1996.

Haglund, Karl. *Inventing the Charles River.* Cambridge, Mass.: The MIT Press, 2003.

Jacobs, S. Quentin. "William Welles Bosworth: Major Works." Master's thesis, Columbia University, 1988.

MacKay, Robert B., Anthony K. Baker, and Carol A. Traynor. *Long Island Country Houses and Their Architects, 1860–1940.* New York: W. W. Norton and the Society for the Preservation of Long Island Antiquities, 1997.

McCash, William Barton, and June Hall McCash. *The Jekyll Island Club: Southern Haven for America's Millionaires.* Athens: University of Georgia Press, 1989.

Pause, Michael. "Teaching the Design Studio, A Case Study: MIT's Department of Architecture, 1865–1974." PhD thesis, MIT Urban Studies, 1977.

Pearson, Henry Greenleaf. *Richard Cockburn Maclaurin, President of the Massachusetts Institute of Technology, 1909–1920.* New York: The Macmillan Co., 1937.

Pierson, Mary Louise. *The Rockefeller Family Home, KyKuit.* Text by Ann Rockefeller Roberts; captions and additional text by Cynthia Altman. New York: Abbeville Press, 1998.

Prescott, Samuel Cate. *When M.I.T. Was "Boston Tech," 1861–1916.* Cambridge, Mass.: Technology Press, 1954.

Schachter, Hindy Lauer. *Frederick Taylor and the Public Administration Community.* Albany: State University of New York Press, 1989.

Shand-Tucci, Douglass. *Built in Boston: City and Suburb, 1800–1950.* Boston: New York Graphic Society, 1978.

Shillaber, Caroline. *Massachusetts Institute of Technology School of Architecture and Planning, 1861–1961: A Hundred Year Chronicle.* Cambridge, Mass.: Massachusetts Institute of Technology, 1963.

Shilland, Kimberly A. "On the Work of Désiré Despradelle." Master's thesis, Boston University, 1989.

Simha, O. Robert. *MIT Campus Planning, 1960–2000, An Annotated Chronology.* Cambridge, Mass.: Massachusetts Institute of Technology, 2001.

Turner, Paul Venable. *Campus: An American Planning Tradition.* Cambridge, Mass.: The MIT Press, 1984.

Wylie, Francis E. *MIT in Perspective, a Pictorial History of the Massachusetts Institute of Technology.* Boston: Little, Brown and Co., 1975.

Illustration Credits

Courtesy of the MIT Museum: 1, 2, 3, 4, 5, 6, 7, 8, 9, 10, 11, 12, 13, 14, 15, 16, 24, 25, 27, 28, 29, 30, 31, 32, 33, 34, 36, 38, 52, 64, 65, 66, 67, 68, 69, 70, 71, 83, 84, 85, 86, 87, 89, 90, 91, 92, 93, 94, 97, 98, 99, 100, 101, 102, 103

MIT Archives: 21, 22, 23, 35, 37, 39, 40, 41, 42, 43, 44, 45, 46, 47, 48, 74

Courtesy of the Harvard University Archives: 17, 18, 26

Courtesy Collection of the New-York Historical Society (negative number 70993): 81

Mark Jarzombek (with permission from Rockefeller Archive Center): 51, 52

Mark Jarzombek: 55, 56, 57, 59, 60, 61, 62, 82, 88, 96

Index